hidden

Finding Delight in Your Life with Christ

ALLISON ALLEN

WITH ASH WIERSMA

Hidden Bible Study Guide

Published in Grand Rapids, Michigan, by HarperChristian Resources. HarperChristian Resources is a registered trademark of HarperCollins Christian Publishing, Inc.

Requests for information should be sent to customercare@harpercollins.com.

ISBN 978-0-310-16125-7 (softcover)
ISBN 978-0-310-16126-4 (ebook)

HarperChristian Resources titles may be purchased in bulk for church, business, fundraising, or ministry use. For information, please e-mail ResourceSpecialist@ChurchSource.com.

Interior images: Oleg Ivanov IL/Shutterstock.com, BibleArtLibrary/iStock.com, Renata Sedmakova/Shutterstock.com

The author is represented by Alive Literary Agency, www.aliveliterary.com.

First Printing October 2023 / Printed in the United States of America

contents

start here

A Note *from* Me to You

To live life is to walk through storms that change us, down to the cellular level. The storm could come disguised as a diagnosis. The agonizing absence of a loved-one. The disappearance of a dearly held friendship or job. A season of depression that won't abate.

I'd be hard-pressed to find someone on earth who hasn't wakened to a typical day only to have her world forever altered by a seemingly benign conversation . . . or who hasn't walked through an unrelenting hurricane that rocked her to her core. Sometimes these seasons are acute and dramatic; sometimes they're cumulative—a slow and agonizing burn. Either way, the result is the same: spiritual grit disappears, and hope begins to dissolve.

Such was the storm I found myself bracing against when I had an unexpected encounter on the shores of the Outer Banks of North Carolina. (I gab about this encounter in session 1.) This storm didn't originate within my family but left us all spun and sputtering nevertheless. Emotionally, we were caught in a riptide. How life itself would be shaped in future days was itself in question.

Looking back, I see that I was no less than depressed—perhaps clinically so. And though I have been anchored in the goodness of God through many an emotional hurricane, the surges of this storm were disorienting in a distinctive way. Still, into this confounding miasma, God spoke to my heart. "I will hand-feed you, child—I will." While I've never heard God's voice audibly, I know that God spoke these words to me. Like a shorebird that had been carried out to sea on a hurricane-force wind and then couldn't find her way back home, I'd been set adrift by my circumstances. Jesus wanted to come to me in my pain and sorrow and nourish me back to health. The question was whether I'd let him.

Would I allow him to tend to my broken heart?

Would I hide myself in the shadow of his wing?

Here's what I want you to know, as you begin this journey with me: God has made good on that promise, 100 percent, *even as my heart is still healing, and not whole yet*. How can both be true simultaneously? I lean into the mystery and paradox of faith. "I believe!" cried the father whose son Jesus had freed from being possessed by an impure spirit. "Help me in my unbelief" (Mark 9:24).

Isn't this how you and I both sometimes feel?

We believe!

And also: *Help us in our unbelief.*

Somehow, within this tension and paradox, God walks alongside us and begins to bring change to our lives. God brings good, God brings healing, God brings insight. What feels catastrophic becomes catalytic. In a season when I felt so hidden in my pain, was it possible that there were treasures to mine? Was there a different way of looking at hiddenness? Was there a different mode of mattering than the one the world says is true?

Though I would never choose it, this most recent painful season I walked through—still am walking through—caused a needed shift in my life regarding how I live out my beliefs about the beauty and bounty to be found in the hidden-with-Christ life.

I don't know what kind of disorientation you've experienced along the way, but if you have survived an unexpected blow that swept you off your feet, or if you've struggled with a sense of invisibility during a tough time, please know that you're not alone. God sees you. God cares for you. God longs to be close to you. And God commits to helping you find your sure footing once again.

Throughout this study, I must report that you won't find any lovely, linear formulas equating your devoted performance with devastation-free days. (Perhaps this is also why you won't find linear sessions, but rather six thematic perspectives on the stunning "seashell" of hiddenness that invite you to turn it gently in the palm of your hand to take in its beauty in varied light.) What you *will* find is my confident testimony that just as a singular wave of the ocean can forcefully cast us adrift, a singular wave of revelation can return us to shore.

My hope for you as you engage with this material is that the storms you've weathered will serve a catalytic purpose for you that prompts you to reflect on aspects of your being that have gone unassessed far too long, to renew your commitment to the One who will never leave you, and to rely on him fully—and solely—for the healing and stunning shelter only he can bring.

With undying hope,

Allison

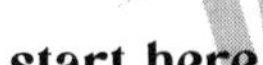

set up for success

Group Facilitator's Guide

Welcome, friend! I'm so glad you're here. I have been on the journey you're embarking on for several years now. I can tell you that you are in for a *real treat* as you learn to hide yourself in God through Christ Jesus and hopefully teach others to do the same.

This work of letting go of the world's perceptions and assessments of us and resting in God's acceptance and admiration instead is the noblest work we can do. Because it is only by his power and provision that we can live the lives he longs for us to live—lives of contentment and curiosity, lives of satisfaction and service, lives of devotedness and determined faithfulness, lives of unwavering and deep-seated *peace.*

Each participant should have his or her own study guide. Each study guide comes with individual streaming video access (instructions found on the inside front cover). Every member of your group has full access to watch videos from the convenience of their chosen devices at any time—for missed group meetings, for rewatching, for sharing teaching with others, or for watching videos individually before meeting if your group is short on meeting time. This gives your group the flexibility to make the experience doable no matter your unique circumstances. We have worked very hard to make gathering around the Word of God and studying it accessible and simple.

Group Selection

This study is intended to be experienced not on your own, but in the context of a group. If you don't already have a group to work through this content with, consider inviting six to eight people from your church, your neighborhood, your friend group, your extended family, or another group you are already associated with to join you.

Prior to your first group meeting, designate the six dates when you will be meeting, so that group members can plan for full participation.

Session Themes

In this six-session experience, you and your group members will be invited to engage with the following concepts:

- Performance culture versus unconditional love
- Visibility versus inherent value
- Earthly accolades versus heavenly reward
- Enslavement to people-pleasing versus freedom in Christ
- Hiding from life versus being hidden in God

Through Bible study, ancient-world callbacks, robust group discussions, corporate and individual prayer, and between-session occasions for self-reflection, repentance, and spiritual growth, you will deepen your appreciation for the fact that because our heavenly Father sees us and accepts us, it matters not what those in the world think.

Session Structure

Sessions are intended to run for 90 minutes each (plus any fellowship time before and/or after each session) and are made up of these segments:

SEGMENT	DURATION	PURPOSE
Session Introduction* A Note on Time and Place The Concealed Character(s)	15 min	Contextualize the session. Introduce the concealed character(s) to be featured.
Group Time Prepare to Watch Play Video Discussion Questions Before You Go	 5 min 20 min 45 min 5 min	Allow time for prayer. Watch video and take notes. Explore group members' perspectives.
Solo Study Day One Day Two Day Three Day Four	[to be completed between group sessions]	Reflect on session content personally for application and further connection.

**Read this section aloud.*

Preparing for Group Sessions

In your role as group facilitator, be sure to tend to the following tasks prior to each session.

Gather Materials

Prior to your first group meeting, be sure each member has the following materials ready to go:

- A copy of this study guide (with streaming video access code on inside front cover)
- Pen
- Bible (quotes are from the New International Version, but any translation will do)
- Access to all six teaching videos. (See inside front cover of study guide or purchase DVD online.)

Ready Your Heart

To maximize your group's time together, commit to spending 30–45 minutes each week preparing not just your materials but your heart for the session to come. This might include:

- Previewing the entire session, perhaps highlighting the discussion questions you want to be sure to save time to address.
- Answering the discussion questions ahead of time, so that if conversation is slow to unfold, you can offer your thoughtful perspective first.
- Reading the broader context surrounding each Bible reference and noting insights you might bring up during group time.
- Praying for each group member by name and texting them a word of encouragement.

Facilitate Group Sessions

During your group's meetings, you will need to take the lead in managing the clock, various group dynamics, and the overall mood. What follows are some tried-and-true tips you might find useful as you work to keep things moving ahead.

1. **Keep time.** Consider designating a timekeeper who will subtly cue you when it's time to move to the next activity or segment of content.
2. **Prep for read-alouds.** There are several segments that are to be read aloud each week but note that not everyone is comfortable reading aloud. Check in with your group members privately before the first session to inquire about their comfort level with reading and/or praying aloud.
3. **Listen well.** Listen more than you talk. Ask follow-up questions whenever group members share poignant insights. Take notes on what people say so that you can reflect on your time together between sessions.
4. **Balance personalities.** Invariably your group will have members who are more comfortable expressing their thoughts and opinions than others. Be careful to (thoughtfully, gently) draw out quiet members and to (tenderly, compassionately) help more exuberant members practice passing the

figurative mic. For quieter types, you might say something such as, "Jane, if you're okay sharing your thoughts on this question, I'll circle back to you after we hear from a few others." Then follow up with Jane after two or three others have answered, to see if she is willing to chime in. For more talkative members, you could say something like, "All right, who else can relate to what Jamie is saying?" This will give you the opportunity to invite discussion from others.

5. **Wait for eight.** Depending on the day, the question at hand, and the personalities involved, you might have occasions when you pose a question and nobody answers. Before you jump in to rescue the situation, wait a full eight seconds. Yes, it will feel like an eternity. But also true, it will be the patient pause someone needs before she is ready to speak.
6. **Accept all input.** It takes courage to speak up in a group setting. Be sure to offer encouragement each time a member shares her insights. Afterward, say, "thank you for sharing that."
7. **Allow for cross-group talk.** During the group discussion, encourage group members to respond to each other without going through you each time.
8. **Practice cross-session weaving.** If you take good notes each week, this will be an easy task to tend to: whenever it makes sense to do so, callback to previous insights made so that your group can start to tie together the various concepts they will encounter during this experience.
9. **Be satisfied with a sampling.** You don't need to hear from every member in response to every question. If one or two people share their thoughts on a specific item and you're ready to move on, go ahead and move on.
10. **Leverage the offline option.** If you can tell that a conversation is veering off-course from the topic at hand, be confident tabling the discussion until later. Say something like, "While this conversation is fascinating, I'm getting the stink-eye from our beloved timekeeper. We'd better move on . . ."
11. **Hold fast to hope.** This experience touches on some deep-seated issues, which in certain cases may cause discussions to feel heavy or hard. Don't be afraid of what's real! But also, be sure to hold fast to hope and to present an optimistic perspective each week.

Thank you!

If you have been walking with Jesus for any length of time, then you already know that what he said about it being far more of a blessing to give than to receive is absolutely, unequivocally *true*. Based on this truth, I wholeheartedly believe that because you have raised your hand and made yourself available to serve your group by facilitating your time together, you will be rewarded in ways that those who aren't serving may not. This is how life with Christ works.

But I would be remiss by not acknowledging that your investment is just that—a *pouring-in* . . . of time and energy and commitment and concern and passion and purpose and love. And for that investment, I thank you. I thank you for showing up. For serving well. And for believing that this journey is not only worth taking but is worth *leading* on others' behalf.

SESSION 1

hidden treasures

Longing to Live Free

"It is for freedom that Christ has set us free. Stand firm, then, and do not let yourselves be burdened again by a yoke of slavery."

GALATIANS 5:1

Session Introduction

15 min.

Ask a group member to read this section aloud as you begin your time together.

We are different people. We have different backgrounds. We come from different families. We assume different things about the world in which we live. We may vote differently, worship differently, dress differently, and order pizza differently, but still this truth remains: *we're all looking for the very same thing.*

We want purpose. We want acceptance. We want some measure of success. We want to know why we're here and then to do that thing well. We want to live—and to know that our life counts.

This explains why we chase one solution after another . . . we're *determined* to reach that goal. Purpose, acceptance, success in life: Just tell us how to get there, and we're sold! The problem is, we can be manipulated so easily. We can set foot on a path that leads us nowhere good.

> *"Even after walking with Jesus for thirty-five years, why do I so often run from the holy hiddenness he offers me and opt for the world's visibility?"*
>
> **ALLISON ALLEN**

In this session, we'll look at the cost of running in the absolute wrong direction to try to find the fulfillment we so desperately seek. What is the effect of believing a lie? Do lies ever deliver on what they so brazenly promise to us?

A Note on Time and Place: City Walls

Ask a group member to read the following section aloud to get your bearings regarding this session's primary biblical account.

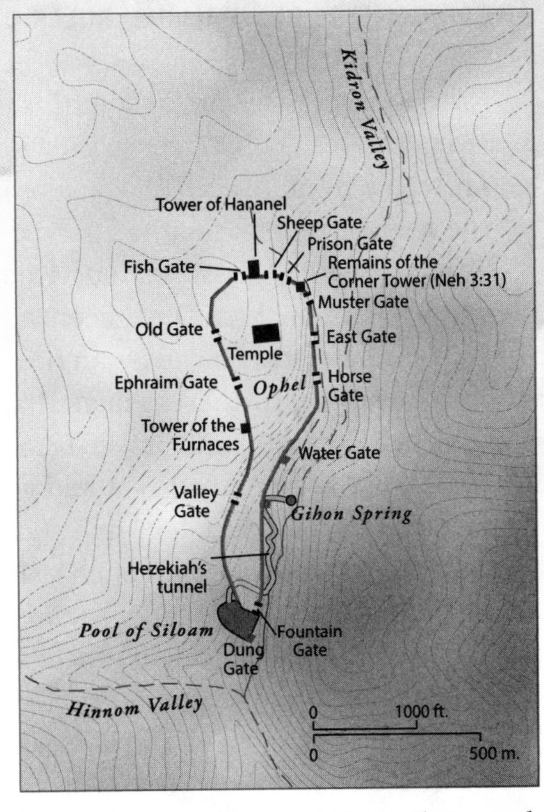

In the ancient world, cities were protected by the physical walls that encircled them, and a breach in one such wall meant that the people who lived within that perimeter were suddenly vulnerable to attack.

About six centuries before the birth of Jesus, the beloved city of Jerusalem—home to the temple that King Solomon had built for God, which remained the most important religious site in Judaism—was attacked by the Babylonians who broke through the city's walls, pillaged and looted the place, and annexed the area as part of their expanding empire.[1]

We learn from 2 Chronicles 32 that in effect, those Babylonian warriors were able to take down the city God loved *by God himself*. You read that right: about a hundred years prior to the attack on Jerusalem, God had tested the heart of Israel's king, King Hezekiah, and found that instead of the king longing for his life to glorify God, Hezekiah longed to gather up glory for himself. Not wise. God stayed his hand for a time but declared that his wrath would one day fall on Judah and Jerusalem. And oh, did it ever.

The story of Nehemiah opens with the results of the king's godless pride: a fortress that had been destroyed in forty-one distinct sections and a people who had all but forgotten their identity in God.

Session 1 Concealed Characters

Ask a group member to read the following Scripture passage aloud, which features this session's "concealed characters."

The Daughters of Shallum, ruler of a half-district of Jerusalem

"The words of Nehemiah son of Hakaliah: In the month of Kislev in the twentieth year, while I was in the citadel of Susa, Hanani, one of my brothers, came from Judah with some other men, and I questioned them about the Jewish remnant that had survived the exile, and also about Jerusalem. They said to me, 'Those who survived the exile and are back in the province are in great trouble and disgrace. The wall of Jerusalem is broken down, and its gates have been burned with fire.'

When I heard these things, I sat down and wept. For some days I mourned and fasted and prayed before the God of heaven. Then I said: 'Lord, the God of heaven, the great and awesome God, who keeps his covenant of love with those who love him and keep his commandments, let your ear be attentive and your eyes open to hear the prayer your servant is praying before you day and night for your servants, the people of Israel. I confess the sins we Israelites, including myself and my father's family, have committed against you. We have acted very wickedly toward you. We have not obeyed the commands, decrees and laws you gave your servant Moses.'

The Jeshanah Gate was repaired by Joiada son of Paseah and Meshullam son of Besodeiah. They laid its beams and put its doors with their bolts and bars in place. Next to them, repairs were made by men from Gibeon and Mizpah—Melatiah of Gibeon and Jadon of Meronoth—places under the authority of the governor of Trans-Euphrates. Uzziel son of Harhaiah, one of the goldsmiths, repaired the next section; and Hananiah, one of the perfume-makers, made repairs next to that. They restored Jerusalem as far as the Broad Wall. Rephaiah son of Hur, ruler of a half-district of Jerusalem, repaired the next section. Adjoining this, Jedaiah son of Harumaph made

> repairs opposite his house, and Hattush son of Hashabneiah made repairs next to him. Malkijah son of Harim and Hasshub son of Pahath-Moab repaired another section and the Tower of the Ovens. **Shallum son of Hallohesh, ruler of a half-district of Jerusalem, repaired the next section with the help of his daughters.**"[2]
>
> **NEHEMIAH 1:1–7; 3:6–12, (EMPHASIS ADDED)**

Group Time

Prepare to Watch: 5 min.

Prior to screening the video segment, spend a few minutes in prayer. The following biblically supported prayer points deal directly with this session's content, but tailor this time to the distinct needs of your group.

Despite the unpredictable and often undesirable circumstances that swirl around us and the indisputable lack of control we possess, you are "the stronghold" of our lives, and thus we need not be afraid **(Psalm 27:1)**.

While our human nature tends toward fretfulness when life unfolds differently than how we hoped or expected it would, we know that as believers we can choose "in every situation, by prayer and petition, with thanksgiving" to present our requests to God **(Philippians 4:6)**.

When we pray instead of pace, when we sit with God instead of spiraling out of sorts, "the peace of God, which transcends all understanding, will guard your hearts and your minds in Christ Jesus" **(Philippians 4:7)**.

The apostle Paul reminds us that "it is for freedom that Christ has set us free" and that by God's power, we can "stand firm" and not let ourselves "be burdened again by a yoke of slavery" **(Galatians 5:1, which is also the epigraph for this session)**.

Play Video Session 1 using streaming code or DVD: 20 min.

Use the space below to log your thoughts or key takeaways from the video teaching.

Wild waters

"You know, the shell is you."

"The shell was beautiful because it had been hidden.
The shell was whole because it had been hidden.
The shell was useful because it had been hidden."

ALLISON ALLEN

Settling for a counterfeit sense of identity

Sacrificing sustenance for the Son of God

Do we want credit or character?

The daughters of Shallum

Fame vs. faithfulness

Delighting in hiddenness

Discussion Questions: 45 min.

Work through the following questions as a group, choosing the ones that are most useful to your group.

1. **Allison mentioned in the video that her family had recently been "tossed" about, prior to their vacationing in the Outer Banks the year she found the intact shell.**

   Can you relate? When have you experienced similar feelings of being set adrift at sea by the circumstances of life?

   Take a minute to capture the memory, and then share your thoughts with your group.

2. **Which ideas about your self-concept, your identity, or your future are you more tempted to believe when you're being "tossed about" by life than when life's seas seem relatively calm?**

   Choose from the list below, or else insert ones that are truer for you. Share your go-to thoughts with the group.

- ☐ "This isn't fair."
- ☐ "Everything is falling apart."
- ☐ "I'm a failure."
- ☐ "Clearly, nobody cares about me."
- ☐ "There's no way out of this."
- ☐ "Nothing good can come from this."
- ☐ "______________________________."
- ☐ "______________________________."
- ☐ "______________________________."

Ask a group member to read this section aloud before continuing your discussion.

It's undeniable that when we believe lies, we suffer as a result. Our relationships with God and others become burdensome, our self-concept becomes confused, our motivation and energy for living life become compromised . . . *everything* takes a hit.

When we're stuck in that downward spiral, any level-headed outside observer would look at our lives and say, "Why doesn't she just . . . stop?"

Stop distancing herself from God.
Stop isolating herself from community.
Stop binge-watching cooking shows.
Stop self-medicating with glass upon glass of wine.
If only we *could* "just stop"!
If only it were as easy as that.

The fact of the matter is that our ability to both *detect* truth and *live according to it* are vehemently, even violently, opposed. We have an enemy, and he is real. If he can keep us from the truth, he can keep us in that "tossed about" state. And it's tough to live uprightly when you're constantly tossed about.

During this session Allison directed our attention to two groups of women who defied the cultural norms of their day to follow God wholeheartedly, in effect "hiding" themselves in him. Have group members look up and read aloud the following sets of verses, and then discuss the questions that follow each passage as a group.

Luke 8:1–3

Here we read of the "many others," women who along with Mary Magdalene; Joanna, the wife of Chuza; and Susanna, Herod's steward, accompanied Jesus as he traveled from village to village, preaching the good news of God's grace.

- In a culture in which women were decidedly less powerful than men,[3] why was it remarkable that these women gave of their own possessions to support Jesus?

- If these women weren't guaranteed any sort of acknowledgement for their devotion and their contribution to Jesus' causes, (and nothing in Scripture says that they were), why do you think they thought it was worth it to sacrifice their sustenance for this work?

Nehemiah 3:9–12

The "daughters of Shallum" assisted in the rebuilding of the walls surrounding the city of Jerusalem, walls that would have still been standing, incidentally, as Jesus made his final entry into that city just before his crucifixion.

- If Shallum's renown could have precluded the man's daughters from engaging in the hard work of helping to rebuild a section of the wall, then why do you suppose they opted in?

- Would you have raised your hand to help with this type of rigorous manual labor when you were a teenager, knowing that you wouldn't be recognized for your hard work? What about now as an adult? Why or why not?

3. **Throughout this series, you might say that the wild waves of the Atlantic are a metaphor for the frenzied, frenetic culture around us that only worsens our sense of destabilization and discontent day by day. As Allison astutely summarized in the video, "we live in a world that equates significance with being seen and excellence with exposure."**

   What evidence of the following "world's-ways" messages do you see infiltrating your own assumptions, attitudes, or actions as you make your way through this season of life? What messages would you add to the list, and how do they influence your ways?

   - [ ] "Busyness is a badge of honor."
   - [ ] "If it doesn't get posted (or tracked), then it didn't happen."
   - [ ] "You are your platform."

- ☐ "Your truth is the only truth that matters. You do you."
- ☐ "Your worth equates to what people think about you."
- ☐ "Your value is determined by where you go, who you're with, and what you do."
- ☐ "______________________________."
- ☐ "______________________________."
- ☐ "______________________________."

> *"We live in a world that equates significance with being seen and excellence with exposure."*
>
> **ALLISON ALLEN**

4. **Thinking back on Allison's experience of walking the beach on the final day of her family's vacation, Allison said that upon finding the intact whelk shell she was reminded of the spiritual truths that she had not been forgotten by God, and that God saw her and her family in their pain. Despite the pain she was enduring, something beautiful lay ahead.**

   When have you been reminded of a supernatural truth as you interacted with the natural world—with something in the wild such as a watercolor sunset, a roaring ocean, a surprise visit from a velvet-antlered deer, a crashing waterfall, a blinding blizzard, a double rainbow, a playful dolphin, the mightiest of thunderstorms, or the tiniest of bugs? What were the circumstances involved and why was the encounter so impactful for you?

5. **What do you make of Allison stumbling upon that shell—sheer coincidence? Divine intervention? Something else? What experiences or assumptions shape your viewpoint here?**

6. **Allison noted three distinctions about that shell that are worth exploring as we come to the end of this session, characteristics that likely explain why her mother-in-law connected the intricate shell directly to her. Because the shell had been hidden for so long, Allison said, it was *beautiful*, it was *whole*, and it was *useful*.**

   We'll work toward making a habit of hiddenness in the coming sessions, but for now, if you were to assess the three aspects of the shell that struck Allison, which do you need most in the season of life you're in today? Select one from the three below, noting your thoughts in the space that follows, and then share your insights with your group.

   - *Beauty*: Being certain of your intrinsic worth and having that divine radiance show up in meaningful ways in your life . . . in your self-assessment, in your attitude, in your ways.

   - *Wholeness*: Living an integrated existence, the kind of life where the gap between *what you believe* and *how you live* gets discernably narrower and narrower over time.

   - *Usefulness*: Impacting the world around you, both today and for generations to come.

Before You Go: 5 min.

Pray as a group through the scriptural truths from each category. Ask God to help you to communicate one of these truths to someone before your group convenes for session 2.

INHERENT WORTH

> "For we are his workmanship, created in Christ Jesus for good works, which God prepared beforehand, that we should walk in them."
>
> **EPHESIANS 2:10, ESV**

INTEGRITY

> "The integrity of the upright guides them, but the crookedness of the treacherous destroys them."
>
> **PROVERBS 11:3, ESV**

IMPACT

> "You are the salt of the earth. But if the salt loses its saltiness, how can it be made salty again? It is no longer good for anything, except to be thrown out and trampled underfoot."
>
> **MATTHEW 5:13**

"Let's follow Jesus, who slipped through the crowds, who told people to tell no one who he was, who spent thirty years in unseen preparation, who came from a no-name backwater town, who pursued not an earthly throne but came for the thorns that would encircle his humble brow. Let's run after this Jesus, who invites us to walk the earth consumed with the king, notoriety, and visibility of the King—and not ourselves."

ALLISON ALLEN

SESSION 1

solo study

Hidden: Finding Delight in Your Life with Christ

Between group sessions, reflect on and dive into the application of the concepts presented in each video across four days.

If there were any group discussion questions your group was unable to get to in your time together, turn back to them and consider them in your personal time as well. Make note of anything you would like to bring up in your next group meeting as you work through this material.

Sink in. See what amazing things unfold. May your time with God be life-giving, productive, and sweet.

solo study

SESSION 1, DAY 1

Truth Statement

My value comes from God.

Read

"Then God said, 'Let us make mankind in our image, in our likeness, so that they may rule over the fish in the sea and the birds in the sky, over the livestock and all the wild animals, and over all the creatures that move along the ground.'

So God created mankind in his own image, in the image of God he created them; male and female he created them. God blessed them and said to them, 'Be fruitful and increase in number, fill the earth and subdue it. Rule over the fish in the sea and the birds in the sky and over every living creature that moves on the ground.'"

GENESIS 1:26–28

Reflect

1. **Think about a specific tumultuous season you've walked through recently. Read the following statement and then take a minute to jot down your thoughts regarding the areas in your life effected by our propensity to believe our circumstances are too dire for hope.**

   When I fall prey to the lie that things are hopeless or, worse still, that I am hopeless, I notice these damaging effects in the various aspects of my life:

   My walk with God:

   My relationships with other people:

   My care for my physical body:

   My energy for my work:

   My influence in my family:

   My thought life:

2. Make a list of the various aspects of your image in the left-hand column. On the right side, jot down the presumed origin of each aspect.

Aspect of My Image	Origin of the Aspect

3. When God thinks of your "image," what thoughts, ideas, assumptions, or words do you suppose come to his mind, and why?

Respond

IMAGE: *tselem*. צֶלֶם. Masculine Noun. (Strong's 6754).
Sounds like: *tzelem*.

Many Bible commentators and interpreters have discussed the meaning of the unique Hebrew word "*tselem*" {צלם} which was translated to English as "image" in Genesis 1:26–27.

The Hebrew word for shadow (*tsel*) comes out of the word *tselem*, and we certainly don't look like shadows, but our shadow behaves exactly like we do. If we jump, so does our shadow; if we wave, our shadow must wave as well. It is an exact replica, a mirrored image of who and what we are. We don't look like it, but we behave like it.

While there are many different Hebrew variables of "image" or *tselem*, consider the depth of purpose in the word *tselem* in Genesis 1:27, as it connects our creation and the shadow of God.[1]

> So God created mankind in his own image,
> in the image of God he created them;
> male and female he created them.
>
> **GENESIS 1:27**

What does it mean to you to think of being God's shadow as described?

How might thinking of yourself in the image of God, as his shadow, in sync with his movements, change your perspective in turbulent or challenging circumstances?

In the spirit of the daughters of Shallum, make a list of services you might complete this week that directs attention to the Source of life—God—instead of to you. Where might your actions be direct reflections of or shadows of God?

1.

2.

3.

4.

5.

Prayer Journal

Consider the prompt below. Complete the sentence as a prayer that reflects your immeasurable worth in Christ.

"Because I am made in your image, God . . ."

solo study

SESSION 1, DAY 2

Truth Statement

I can act on what I believe.

Read

"Do not merely listen to the word, and so deceive yourselves. Do what it says. Anyone who listens to the word but does not do what it says is like someone who looks at his face in a mirror and, after looking at himself, goes away and immediately forgets what he looks like.

But whoever looks intently into the perfect law that gives freedom, and continues in it—not forgetting what they have heard, but doing it—they will be blessed in what they do."

JAMES 1:22–25

Reflect

1. **If someone were to ask you about the values that are most important to you, which ones would you rattle off? Quality time with your family? Wise financial stewardship? Daily prayer? Conscientiousness in your work? Jot down your thoughts below.**

2. **On a scale of 1 to 10, with 10 equating a perfect score, how would you rate your consistency these days in living up to the values that you listed?**

1 — 2 — 3 — 4 — 5 — 6 — 7 — 8 — 9 — 10

3. **Try to identify what is either holding you back or what might be spurring you on.**

   Name it here:____________________.

   If it is holding you back, follow it up with a statement of how you will seek to overcome the barrier: ____.

   If it is spurring you on, claim that encouragement over some lesser motivated areas in your life: ____.

"One might imagine that the daughters of Shallum could have opted out, but there they are, the only women listed in the book of Nehemiah bearing those biceps, heave ho-ing those great stones, rebuilding, restoring the heritage of God's people. What were their names? We don't know. We just know that they were faithful."

ALLISON ALLEN

Respond

It is said that with each choice we make in our daily lives, we're casting a vote for the people we long to be tomorrow, and for all the tomorrows after that. It's true: habits are formed day by day and decision by decision as we determine in our minds, in our hearts, and with our hands who we will become.

Most people wouldn't have been able to answer the question about how well they live out their highest-priority values with a perfect 10. We all have room to grow. And it's clear from the testimony of Scripture that God longs to help us do just that.

In the story of the daughters of Shallum, we see that the way they spent a mere fifty-plus days of their life—the amount of time it took to rebuild the protective walls of Jerusalem—became the basis for their legacy, for how their lives would count for all time.

If you were to take a single step of action today that would help close the gap ever so slightly between the person you are and the person you long to be, a step that might just become a week-long habit and then a month-long habit and then a fifty-three-day habit and then an automatic and beneficial part of your life,

What would that step be, and why would you take it?

More importantly, will you take that step today?

Prayer Journal

Consider the prompt below. Complete the sentence as a prayer that reflects your desire to be a shadow image of our Creator God.

"By your power, Father . . ."

solo study

SESSION 1, DAY 3

Truth Statement

God wants me to cooperate with his plans.

Read

"For the eyes of the LORD range throughout the earth to strengthen those whose hearts are fully committed to him."

2 CHRONICLES 16:9

Reflect

1. **If your family members or closest friends were asked about the biggest commitments in your life, the obligations or involvements that you tend to build your days around, which commitments would they name?**

2. **What do you make of the fact that there is more of God available to those whose number-one commitment is to him? The more of him you seek and prioritize, the more of him you receive. Make a short list of ways you can prioritize time with God over all other commitments this week (and moving forward).**

Respond

Throughout the Bible, we see that God loves to leverage the talents and training of his people by giving them opportunities to serve. And that those who are devoted to him are secure and confident to say yes when those opportunities arise, because they recognize his leading and positioning and call.

Today, spend your remaining time asking God for input regarding how you might fulfill a commitment not of your own making but of his. If he were building your schedule today, what to-do's would show up in the slots?

Note any insights you receive, as you sit before him and listen.

Prayer Journal

Consider the prompt. Complete the sentence and journal a prayer that reflects your desire to be a clear image of God.

"Lord, as you look for those who are committed to you . . ."

solo study

SESSION 1, DAY 4

Truth Statement

Eternal wealth is more fulfilling than earthly wealth pretends to be.

Read

"Do not store up for yourselves treasures on earth, where moths and vermin destroy, and where thieves break in and steal. But store up for yourselves treasures in heaven, where moths and vermin do not destroy, and where thieves do not break in and steal. For where your treasure is, there your heart will be also."

MATTHEW 6:19–21

Reflect

1. **What earthly "treasures" most often distract you from offering your full devotion to God?**

2. **Do you consider yourself "spiritually wealthy"? Why, or why not?**

Respond

We understand from extrabiblical writings that the daughters of Shallum were materially wealthy women, but based on the Nehemiah account, we suspect there was more to their story than that.

What evidence of *spiritual* wealth do you detect in the daughters' story that you could demonstrate in your own life today?

> *"God has untold blessings in store for us as we pursue hiddenness in Christ."*
>
> ALLISON ALLEN

Prayer Journal

Consider the prompt. Complete the sentence and journal a prayer that reflects your acknowledgement of the all-satisfying provision of God.

"You are my Provider, God, . . ."

SESSION 2

where all good things are found

Residing in God's Sufficiency

"Set your minds on things above, not on earthly things. For you died, and your life is now hidden with Christ in God. When Christ, who is your life, appears, then you also will appear with him in glory."

COLOSSIANS 3:2–4

"Hide yourself in my win . . ."

Session Introduction

15 min.

Ask a group member to read this section aloud as you begin your time together.

Who doesn't love a "secret formula"? Marketing geniuses know that to sell a product or service, all they need to do is convince us unsuspecting consumers that we are missing out on some super-secret, super-special, super-spectacular thing, and we will spend or sign up or subscribe in a heartbeat.

How often do these hyped products and services deliver on what they promise to do? Never. How often do we keep falling for those promises, despite our knowing how often they fail? Over and over again. Because *this* time, we're sure it will work. Maddening, right?

The message that the apostle Paul conveyed to believers in Colossae hits our modern ears as *utter relief*. We don't have to keep searching for some secret formula in life. All that we need is found in Christ.

> *"There is no secret, hidden knowledge reserved for special people here on earth. There is nothing greater to be understood than the mystery that has been fully and finally revealed through and in Jesus Christ."*
>
> **ALLISON ALLEN**

In the last session, we looked at the perils of believing lies. In this session, we'll explore what happens when we believe the truth . . . plus something more. *Syncretism*, it's called, this "Jesus-plus" approach to life.[1] It's the refusal to accept the gospel of Jesus Christ as God intended it to be: freely given, freely received, via wholehearted faith in God (see Ephesians 2:8–10). And it's simply devastating in its effects.

To "hide ourselves in Christ" is to look to him, alone, for protection. For provision. For contentment. For sufficiency. For hope. And for the ultimate victory—the conquering of death by life. The earthly things we keep falling for cannot deliver what heaven boasts, which is why the choice is set before us in Colossians: will we wed ourselves to the "elemental" things of this world, or to the Savior, the risen Christ?

A Note on Time and Place: The Emmaus Road

Ask a group member to read the following section aloud to get your bearings regarding this session's primary biblical account.

To be a faithful Jew in the first century was to be well-acquainted with worship. In Exodus 12, we read of God handing down instruction to his people regarding when they were to pause in the midst of their work and life and give honor to him. Three major feasts led the way: the Feast of Unleavened Bread, also known as Passover or Pesach; the Feast of Weeks, also known as Pentecost or Shavout; and the Feast of Booths, or Sukkoth.[2]

Jews living on the outskirts of town would often make the trek to the temple mount in Jerusalem on these and other high, holy days, which is likely why we find the two disciples traveling from Jerusalem back to their home in Emmaus following Jesus' crucifixion.

Scholars differ on the second disciple's identity—was it another of "the twelve," such as Luke or James? Was it someone Jesus had encountered during his earthly ministry, such as Simon or Nicodemus? Was it in fact Mary, mother of James and Cleopas's wife? Whoever it was, we know that Cleopas and his traveling companion were grieving as they departed the city.[3] The Messiah they'd had such high hopes for had been brutally murdered on a Roman cross, while onlookers ridiculed him and all who associated with him. As they slowly made their way along the dirt path dotted by ancient paving stones, a seven-mile trek in all, they surely shared feelings of being perplexed over all that had unfolded.

Session 2 Concealed Character

Ask a group member to read the following Scripture passage aloud, which features this session's "concealed character."

Cleopas, one of the two disciples on the road to Emmaus

"Now that same day [on the day of Jesus' resurrection] two of them [the disciples] were going to a village called Emmaus, about seven miles from Jerusalem. They were talking with each other about everything that had happened. As they talked and discussed these things with each other, Jesus himself came up and walked along with them; but they were kept from recognizing him.

He asked them, 'What are you discussing together as you walk along?'

They stood still, their faces downcast. One of them, named Cleopas, asked him, 'Are you the only one visiting Jerusalem who does not know the things that have happened there in these days?'

'What things?' he asked.

'About Jesus of Nazareth,' they replied. 'He was a prophet, powerful in word and deed before God and all the people. The chief priests and our rulers handed him over to be sentenced to death, and they crucified him; but we had hoped that he was the one who was going to redeem Israel. And what is more, it is the third day since all this took place. In addition, some of our women amazed us. They went to the tomb early this morning but didn't find his body. They came and told us that they had seen a vision of angels, who said he was alive. Then some of our companions went to the tomb and found it just as the women had said, but they did not see Jesus.'

He said to them, 'How foolish you are, and how slow to believe all that the prophets have spoken! Did not the Messiah have to suffer these things and then enter his glory?' And beginning with Moses and all the Prophets, he explained to them what was said in all the Scriptures concerning himself.

As they approached the village to which they were going, Jesus continued on as if he were going farther. But they urged him strongly, 'Stay with us, for it is nearly evening; the day is almost over.' So he went in to stay with them.

When he was at the table with them, he took bread, gave thanks, broke it and began to give it to them. Then their eyes were opened and they recognized him, and he disappeared from their sight. They asked each other, 'Were not our hearts burning within us while he talked with us on the road and opened the Scriptures to us?'

They got up and returned at once to Jerusalem. There they found the Eleven and those with them, assembled together and saying, 'It is true! The Lord has risen and has appeared to Simon.' Then the two told what had happened on the way, and how Jesus was recognized by them when he broke the bread."

LUKE 24:13–35

Group Time

Prepare to Watch: 5 min.

Prior to screening the video segment, spend a few minutes in prayer. The following biblically supported prayer points deal directly with this session's content, but tailor this time to the distinct needs of your group.

Despite the world's claims that what matters most in life is that which we can experience with our five senses, for believers "we walk by faith, not by sight" (2 Corinthians 5:7, ESV).

When we're "in Christ," we are equipped with everything we need to keep "in step with the Spirit" (Galatians 5:25). This means we can live successfully, over time—over a *lifetime*, even—according to the will of God.

What awaits those who are in Christ is an eternity spent with God. According to 1 Peter 1:3–5, in God's great mercy, "he has given us new birth into a living hope through the resurrection of Jesus Christ from the dead, and into an inheritance that can never perish, spoil or fade. This inheritance is kept in heaven for you, who through faith are shielded by God's power until the coming of the salvation that is ready to be revealed in the last time." *Ultimate* victory over *ultimate* death—this is what awaits.

Play Video Session 2 using streaming code or DVD: 21 min.

Use the space below to log your thoughts or key takeaways from the video teaching.

Unimportant and obscure

The Colossae Controversy

Minding our mix

Is there anywhere in your life that the Holy Spirit is illuminating for you, where you might need to mind your mix? The grace of Jesus plus a little law, Jesus plus a little superstition, Jesus plus fill-in-the-blank . . .

Kept and protected by Christ

"Don't look down!"

Stripped to the studs

Jesus' patient reveal

"With Christ, we are hidden with someone so much better, so much bigger . . . He is the all-in-all."

ALLISON ALLEN

Seeing Christ for who he is

Discussion Questions: 45 min.

> **Work through the following questions as a group, choosing the ones that are most useful to your group.**

1. **In the video segment, Allison talked about our human-nature tendency down through the ages to adopt a syncretistic approach to our spiritual lives. Believers more than two thousand years ago struggled with this temptation, and we struggle with it still today.**

   Think of a time when you have fallen for a "Jesus-plus" way of living. What was the "plus" you tried to add to the sufficiency of Christ? See if any of the following prompts resonate with you. If not, add your own to the list.

   - ☐ *Jesus plus* good deeds.
   - ☐ *Jesus plus* financial generosity.
   - ☐ *Jesus plus* perfect attendance.
   - ☐ *Jesus plus* over-functioning.
   - ☐ *Jesus plus* self-denial.
   - ☐ *Jesus plus* "acting right."
   - ☐ *Jesus plus* ______________________________

   Why is "Jesus plus" anything—even a good and noble thing—a dangerous proposition?

2. Ask a group member to read aloud Paul's words in Colossians 2:6–8 (see callout). Then answer the following questions together:

- What imagery does Paul use in explaining what it's like to believe "hollow and deceptive philosophy"? Why do you think he chose this imagery?

- Why do you think Paul is so concerned about followers of Jesus depending on "human tradition"? Why is that such a bad thing?

- Ask a group member to look up and read aloud a portion of another of Paul's letters found in Romans 6:16–18. What are believers *supposed* to be slaves to?

> "So then, just as you received Christ Jesus as Lord, continue to live your lives in him, rooted and built up in him, strengthened in the faith as you were taught, and overflowing with thankfulness. See to it that no one takes you captive through hollow and deceptive philosophy, which depends on human tradition and the elemental spiritual forces of this world rather than on Christ."
>
> —COLOSSIANS 2:6–8

3. **During the video, Allison exhorted us to "mind our mix" as it relates to assessing whether we are living for something real. Spend a few minutes pondering the assumptions, attitudes, thought patterns, areas of entitlement, habits, or actions that you suspect might not fit into a life that is fully surrendered—fully in bondage—to the lordship of Jesus Christ.**

   What might have to go, in other words, if you want to not be a "Jesus-plus" but a "Jesus-only" kind of person?

   After you jot down your thoughts based on the following categories, share an insight you made with your group.

   Errant assumptions . . .

   Selfish attitudes . . .

   Unhelpful thought patterns . . .

   Stubborn entitlements . . .

Soul-squelching habits . . .

Absurd actions . . .

Ask a group member to read this section aloud before continuing your discussion.

In a culture that has conditioned us to believe that we can hustle our way to acceptance, charm our way into good graces, and grind our way to the top, it's almost inconceivable that the truth of the matter according to our heavenly Father is that the only thing we need to do is *receive.*

It's preposterous to our twenty-first century developed-world ears to hear that the single-greatest priority we can hold in life is to hide ourselves instead of clawing our way to be seen.

But there it is, the truth of the gospel, the news that seems too good to be true. The Son really is the firstborn of all creation, the image of the invisible God. In Jesus, all things really were created, things both in heaven and here on earth. By his mighty grip, God really does hold all things together, including—scandalously—you and me. We really can tuck ourselves into his all-sufficient presence and power . . . and therein find all that we need.[4]

4. **What negative connotations regarding the concept of *hiddenness* do you carry today that you'd like to get off your chest? What fears rise in you when you consider "hiding" yourself in Christ?**

5. **On the flip side of question 4, what opportunities, advantages, benefits, or consolations do you suspect you might realize going forward if you were to faithfully hide yourself in him?**

> *"Because of Jesus' great work, we're safe emotionally, eternally, positionally, actually. That does something for me. When the world tempts me to make a name for myself or add some secret system to my faith, I want somebody to protect me, to guard me, and to hide me. That person is Jesus."*

ALLISON ALLEN

Before You Go: 5 min.

Pray as a group through the scriptural truths below from each category. Ask God to help you to communicate one of these truths to someone before your group convenes for session 3.

INVITATION

"He told them, 'The secret of the kingdom of God has been given to you.'"

MARK 4:11

REVELATION

"But when he, the Spirit of truth, comes, he will guide you into all the truth."

JOHN 16:13

TRANSFORMATION

"And we all, who with unveiled faces contemplate the Lord's glory, are being transformed into his image with ever-increasing glory, which comes from the Lord, who is the Spirit."

2 CORINTHIANS 3:18

"Because of Jesus' sacrifice on the cross, we are held apart, kept and protected in an eternal way with Christ. Our very life, our true life, our eternal life, is buried with him. We're tucked in. We're hidden. We're safe."

ALLISON ALLEN

SESSION 2

solo study

Hidden: Finding Delight in Your Life with Christ

Between group sessions, reflect on and dive into the application of the concepts presented in each video across four days.

If there were any group discussion questions your group was unable to get to in your time together, turn back to them and consider them in your personal time as well. Make note of anything you would like to bring up in your next group meeting as you work through this material.

Sink in. See what amazing things unfold. May your time with God be life-giving, productive, and sweet.

solo study

SESSION 2, DAY 1

Truth Statement

God has invited me into relationship with him.

Read

"He has saved us and called us to a holy life—not because of anything we have done but because of his own purpose and grace.

This grace was given us in Christ Jesus before the beginning of time, but it has now been revealed through the appearing of our Savior, Christ Jesus, who has destroyed death and has brought life and immortality to light through the gospel."

2 TIMOTHY 1:9–10

Reflect

1. **What thoughts or emotions come to mind as you sit with the reality that God's grace has been waiting on you since "before the beginning of time"?**

2. **Are you pleased with how you have responded to and stewarded the gift of grace that God has offered you? Why, or why not? What would need to be true of your life for you to give a resounding *yes*?**

Respond

It has been said that the depiction of the disciples walking deflated and demoralized to Emmaus only to head right back to Jerusalem hours later filled with *burning hearts* that had been reignited by Jesus himself is the perfect picture of salvation's journey.

What demoralizing situation are you facing today that might be altogether recast in light of Jesus' great sacrifice on your behalf? Through prayer, would you be willing to invite him into that challenge now? If so, work through the following prompts, and in so doing, remind your faltering heart that in Christ, you have all the protection, all the provision, all the hope, all the *victory* that a person could need.

Heavenly Father, I can relate to those disciples who walked the road to Emmaus feeling heartbroken and in pain. As I walk this stretch of my own life's journey, the source of my disillusionment is this:

I survey this scene and feel:

And those feelings make me wonder if:

In the same way that those disciples experienced your presence in a tangible way, I humbly ask you to be near to me in a way that I can perceive. In your nearness, please help me to see:

And to hear:

And to feel:

And to believe:

Keep me on the path, Lord. I pray in Jesus' holy name,

Amen.

Prayer Journal

Consider the prompt below. Complete the sentence as a prayer recognizing that God is always near and here with you.

"Because I have said yes to you, God . . ."

solo study

SESSION 2, DAY 2

Truth Statement

The Holy Spirit will guide me into all truth.

Read

"But when he, the Spirit of truth, comes, he will guide you into all the truth. He will not speak on his own; he will speak only what he hears, and he will tell you what is yet to come."

JOHN 16:13

Reflect

1. **What sources of "guidance" are you most closely following these days?**

2. **What does it mean to you that God refers to his Spirit as the "Spirit of truth"?**

Respond

We see in Luke 24:13–35 the disciples who encountered the risen Christ on the road to Emmaus realize in whose presence they stood, and some pretty significant exchanges were made. Because of Jesus they were able to trade sorrow for celebration. They were able to trade confusion for clarity. They were able to trade disillusionment for deep-seated contentment.

Jesus is near. He is near to you now. What exchanges are you desiring to make?

This	for	That

Prayer Journal

Consider the prompt. Complete the sentence and journal a prayer that reflects your proclamation to walk in truth, no matter the many ways this world attempts to counter the will of the Lord.

"By your Spirit, . . ."

solo study

SESSION 2, DAY 3

Truth Statement

By God's power, I can become more like Jesus each day.

Read

"Follow God's example, therefore, as dearly loved children and walk in the way of love, just as Christ loved us and gave himself up for us as a fragrant offering and sacrifice to God."

EPHESIANS 5:1–2

Reflect

1. **When you think about "God's example," what character attributes, postures of heart, or actions come to mind?**

2. **When your life is *most* scented like the "fragrance of Christ," what thoughts are you thinking? What habits are you practicing? What dreams are you dreaming?**

Respond

Read Luke 24:13–35 again. As soon as Jesus revealed his identity to the disciples on the road to Emmaus, those disciples wasted no time in getting back to Jerusalem to tell others about the truth of Jesus' resurrection. Who in your life would benefit from hearing your story of encountering Jesus and being changed by the sacrifice he made on your behalf?

What is standing in the way of your telling him or her?

Prayer Journal

Consider the prompt below. Complete the sentence as a prayer that reflects your own hiddenness in Christ.

"*I am alive in Christ . . .*"

solo study

SESSION 2, DAY 4

Truth Statement

I need nothing, apart from Christ.

Read

"Such confidence we have through Christ before God. Not that we are competent in ourselves to claim anything for ourselves, but our competence comes from God.

He has made us competent as ministers of a new covenant—not of the letter but of the Spirit; for the letter kills, but the Spirit gives life."

2 CORINTHIANS 3:4–6

Reflect

1. **As you survey your life patterns today, do you tend to rely more on your self-made competence or on the competence that comes from God? What evidence supports your insight here?**

2. **What do you suppose is true for someone whose competence wholly comes from God?**

Respond

In the spirit of "minding your mix," what are two practical ways you can cede control of your circumstances, obligations, hopes and dreams, and to-do's to the lordship of Jesus today?

1. ______________________________

2. ______________________________

Prayer Journal

Consider the prompt below. Complete the sentence as a prayer that reflects your confidence in the Lord.

"Such confidence I have in you, Lord, because . . ."

SESSION 3

choosing excellence over exposure

Receiving the Gifts of God's Truth

"How can a young person stay on the path of purity?
By living according to your word.
I seek you with all my heart;
do not let me stray from your commands.
I have hidden your word in my heart
that I might not sin against you."

PSALM 119:9–11

"Hide yourself in my Word . . ."

Session Introduction

15 min.

Ask a group member to read this section aloud as you begin your time together.

If you were able to see inside of your heart—inside the seat of your emotions and inclinations and affections and dreams—what do you suppose you'd find there? Does the mere thought of such an endeavor send a shiver up your spine? Be not afraid. We can't actually accomplish this task. But it's a good thought experiment considering what is contained in our hearts. Surely there is a jumble of things present: both frustrations and contentment; both anxiety and peace; both hilarity and deep sorrow; perspective and meltdown there, side-by-side.

Perhaps the more productive experiment is this one: Were you able to peek inside your heart, what would you *hope* to find there? Or better yet: what does our heavenly Father hope to find when he looks inside our hearts?

Throughout the Scriptures, we find all sorts of clues regarding the life God longs for us to live, and what that life will mean for the state of our hearts. There are exhortations to *write God's will* on our hearts and to *keep his ways* on our hearts and to *hold God's wisdom close* to our living, beating hearts. "Fix these words of mine in your hearts and minds," God says through his leader Moses in Deuteronomy 11:18, "tie them as symbols on your hands and bind them on your foreheads."

There's this, from King Solomon, widely considered the wisest man ever to live: "Let love and faithfulness never leave you; bind them around your neck, write them on the tablet of your heart" (Proverbs 3:3).

And then this, from the writer of Hebrews (whom most consider to be the apostle Paul): "This is the covenant I will establish with the people of Israel after that time, declares the Lord. I will put my laws in their minds and write them on their hearts. I will be their God, and they will be my people" (Hebrews 8:10).

It's interesting imagery, don't you think? Of course, we can't *actually* write on our hearts. But in the same way that you could engrave metal such that the marks would remain as an everlasting impression, it's as though God is saying, "I want you to etch my *ideas* and my *ideals* onto the deepest part of your life so that whenever you need wisdom, wisdom will be near."

Importantly, we read in 2 Chronicles 16:9 that there is a real benefit to living this way. There, Hanani issues this key reminder: "For the eyes of the LORD range throughout the earth to strengthen those whose hearts are fully committed to him."

Now to the most critical piece of information of all: *how we can practically get this done.*

In this session, we'll assess what happens in the hearts of believers when they accept God's profound invitation to hide themselves in his Word, the Holy Scriptures, source of divine insight, instruction, inspiration.[1] As the psalmist David declared in Psalm 119:11, it is only when we put God's Word inside our hearts that we can avoid sinning against him.

A Note on Time and Place: The Book of the Law

> **Ask a group member to read the following section aloud to get your bearings regarding this session's primary biblical account.**

When the Bible mentions the "Book of the Law," it is referring to the Old Testament book of Deuteronomy—the first twenty-nine chapters, anyway—which was an expansion of the Ten Commandments and kept beside the Ark of the Covenant. (The Ten Commandments themselves were kept inside the ark.)[2]

This "Book" contained what is known as the "second law," or a restatement of the Ten Commandments that Moses was given by God as he endeavored to lead the nation Israel along the path of righteousness and was written on a parchment scroll. When we read in this session's featured text that Hilkiah has "found the Book of the Law" (2 Chronicles 34:15), this turn of events is significant because of the Book having been misplaced during the previous kings' reigns.

The words we find in Deuteronomy today are the same as the ones that this session's concealed character, Huldah, would have affirmed, except that they were written in Hebrew instead of English and did not include chapter and verse designations. Those would be added nearly two thousand years later during the Middle Ages.

Session 3 Concealed Character

Ask a group member to read the following Scripture passage aloud, which features this session's "concealed character."

Huldah the Prophetess

"Josiah was eight years old when he began to reign, and he reigned thirty-one years in Jerusalem. And he did what was right in the eyes of the Lord, and walked in the ways of David his father; and he did not turn aside to the right hand or to the left. For in the eighth year of his reign, while he was yet a boy, he began to seek the God of David his father, and in the twelfth year he began to purge Judah and Jerusalem of the high places, the Asherim, and the carved and the metal images. And they chopped down the altars of the Baals in his presence, and he cut down the incense altars that stood above them. And he broke in pieces the Asherim and the carved and the metal images, and he made dust of them and scattered it over the graves of those who had sacrificed to them.

He also burned the bones of the priests on their altars and cleansed Judah and Jerusalem. And in the cities of Manasseh, Ephraim, and Simeon, and as far as Naphtali, in their ruins all around, he broke down the altars and beat the Asherim and the images into powder and cut down all the incense altars throughout all the land of Israel. Then he returned to Jerusalem.

Now in the eighteenth year of his reign, when he had cleansed the land and the house, he sent Shaphan the son of Azaliah, and Maaseiah the governor of the city, and Joah the son of Joahaz, the recorder, to repair the house of the LORD his God.

They came to Hilkiah the high priest and gave him the money that had been brought into the house of God, which the Levites, the keepers of the threshold, had collected from Manasseh and Ephraim and from all the remnant of Israel and from all Judah and Benjamin and from the inhabitants of Jerusalem. And they gave it to the workmen who were working in the house of the LORD. And the workmen who were working in the house of the LORD gave it for repairing and restoring the house. They gave it to the carpenters and the builders to buy quarried stone, and timber for binders and beams for the buildings that the kings of Judah had let go to ruin.

And the men did the work faithfully. Over them were set Jahath and Obadiah the Levites, of the sons of Merari, and Zechariah and Meshullam, of the sons of the Kohathites, to have oversight. The Levites, all who were skillful with instruments of music, were over the burden-bearers and directed all who did work in every kind of service, and some of the Levites were scribes and officials and gatekeepers.

While they were bringing out the money that had been brought into the house of the LORD, Hilkiah the priest found the Book of the Law of the LORD given through Moses. Then Hilkiah answered and said to Shaphan the secretary, 'I have found the Book of the Law in the house of the LORD." And Hilkiah gave the book to Shaphan.

Shaphan brought the book to the king, and further reported to the king, 'All that was committed to your servants they are doing. They have emptied out the money that was found in the house of the LORD and have given it into the hand of the overseers and the workmen.'

Then Shaphan the secretary told the king, 'Hilkiah the priest has given me a book.' And Shaphan read from it before the king.

And when the king heard the words of the Law, he tore his clothes. And the king commanded Hilkiah, Ahikam the son of Shaphan, Abdon the son of Micah, Shaphan the secretary, and Asaiah the king's servant, saying, 'Go, inquire of the LORD for me and for those who are left in Israel and in Judah, concerning the words of the book that has been found. For great is the wrath of the LORD that is poured out on us, because our fathers have not kept the word of the LORD, to do according to all that is written in book.'

So Hilkiah and those whom the king had sent went to Huldah the prophetess, the wife of Shallum the son of Tokhath, son of Hasrah, keeper of the wardrobe (now she lived in Jerusalem in the Second Quarter) and spoke to her to that effect.

And she said to them, 'Thus says the LORD, the God of Israel: "Tell the man who sent you to me, Thus says the LORD, Behold, I will bring disaster upon this place and upon its inhabitants, all the curses that are written in the book that was read before the king of Judah. Because they have forsaken me and have made offerings to other gods, that they might provoke me to anger with all the works of their hands, therefore my wrath will be poured out on this place and will not be quenched. But to the king of Judah, who sent you to inquire of the LORD, thus shall you say to him, Thus says the LORD, the God of Israel: Regarding the words that you have heard, because your heart was tender and you humbled yourself before God when you heard his words against this place and its inhabitants, and you have humbled yourself before me and have torn your clothes and wept before me, I also have heard you, declares the LORD. Behold, I will gather you to your fathers, and you shall be gathered to your grave in peace, and your eyes shall not see all the disaster that I will bring upon this place and its inhabitants."'

And they brought back word to the king.

Then the king sent and gathered together all the elders of Judah and Jerusalem. And the king went up to the house of the LORD, with all the men of Judah and the inhabitants of Jerusalem and the priests and the Levites, all the people both great and small. And he read in their hearing all the words of the Book of the Covenant that had been found in the house of the LORD.

And the king stood in his place and made a covenant before the LORD, to walk after the LORD and to keep his commandments and his testimonies and his statutes, with all his heart and all his soul, to perform the words of the covenant that were written in this book.

> Then he made all who were present in Jerusalem and in Benjamin join in it. And the inhabitants of Jerusalem did according to the covenant of God, the God of their fathers. And Josiah took away all the abominations from all the territory that belonged to the people of Israel and made all who were present in Israel serve the Lord their God. All his days they did not turn away from following the Lord, the God of their fathers."
>
> **2 CHRONICLES 34:1–33, ESV (EMPHASIS ADDED)**

Group Time

Prepare to Watch: 5 min.

Prior to screening the video segment, spend a few minutes in prayer. The following scripturally supported prayer points deal directly with this session's content, but tailor this time to the distinct needs of the members in your group.

Despite the circumstances that are challenging us, confronting us, and possibly causing chaos in our lives, we know that because we are children of God, "under his wings" we "will find refuge" **(Psalm 91:4)**.

Even when we are imperfect in our followership of Jesus, we can become like David, who was described as a "man after his [God's] own heart" **(1 Samuel 13:14)**.

When we "humble ourselves," allowing God to promote us instead of fighting to promote ourselves, our promotion will happen "in due time" **(1 Peter 5:6)**.

As followers of Christ, we don't have to *fret over* or *force* fruitfulness. It is God who "cuts off every branch" in us that bears no fruit, "while every branch that does bear fruit he prunes so that it will be even more fruitful" **(John 15:2)**.

Play Video Session 3 using streaming code or DVD: 21 min.

Use the space below to log your thoughts or key takeaways from the video teaching.

Hidden on purpose for a purpose

Moses' long, hidden season

Quiet, concealed years have the effect of washing off false modes of being, counterfeit ways of coping, reducing us to the essentials of who we actually are. The hidden years cause a great and necessary stripping away. A loss of what cannot remain for a gain that cannot be lost.

Jesus' solitude

When God tends to speak

Gift #1: Preparation

Gift #2: Protection

Gift #3: Potency

Gift #4: Perfect Timing

Discussion Questions: 45 min.

Work through the following questions as a group, choosing the ones that are most useful to your group.

1. **When have you experienced an episode or a season of unexpected hiddenness in your life? What circumstances converged to usher in that time in your life? Furthermore, how did you feel about being hidden? With hindsight as your filter, how does the occasion sit in your memory now?**

   Give these questions some thought. Then, after jotting down notes from that occasion below, share your insights with your group.

2. **What thoughts or feelings rise to the surface for you as you take in Allison's observation that God "has a penchant for hiding his people purposefully now for purpose later on"?**

   What do you suppose was the purpose for the occasion of hiddenness you described in response to the last question?

3. **Would you say you're more prone to viewing times of hiddenness as punishment or as reward? What firsthand experiences or pervading assumptions back your belief do you suppose?**

4. **Along these lines, why do you suppose so many believers assume that when God "hid" various people in Scripture for long periods of time—the apostle Paul for two or three years, Joseph for a dozen or more years, Jesus for thirty years, Moses for forty—he did so for really important reasons, but that when he "hides" us for even *one moment* beyond our comfort level, he is doing so out of spite?**

Ask a group member to read this section aloud before continuing your discussion.

Throughout Scripture, we see two themes emerge: man's glory and how it leads to destruction, and God's glory and how it leads to the redemption of all things. As we saw in session 2, we can't pursue both aims at the same time. We must *devote ourselves fully to Jesus*, or by definition we have elevated our own will and ways above God's.

To follow Jesus is to prize what he prized. To prioritize what he prioritized. To glorifying only what he glorified. To love as Jesus loved.[3]

"We so often confuse human affirmation with the King's holy kiss."

ALLISON ALLEN

5. **During the video, Allison posed a pair of rhetorical questions that are worth answering outright: "What if we showed up to the moments that the Lord presented to us," she asked, "stepping into the spotlight of his story long enough to serve, and then fading away just as effortlessly into obscurity? What if we sought hiddenness?"**

Ask a group member to read the above quote aloud and then sit with the following questions before sharing a few of your insights with the rest of the group.

What type of person could adopt this type of "Huldah approach" to life? What character traits would such a person possess?

Which of these character traits do I see in my life today? Which do I lack?

What's the difference between contriving opportunities for "being in the spotlight" versus cooperating with God when he chooses to place me there?

"What would happen if we invited God to purge us of the need to be seen?"

ALLISON ALLEN

Before You Go: 5 min.

Pray as a group through the scriptural truths below from each category. Ask God to help you to communicate one of these truths to someone before your group convenes for session 4.

PREPARATION

"Commit to the LORD whatever you do, and he will establish your plans. The LORD works out everything to its proper end—even the wicked for a day of disaster."

PROVERBS 16:3–4

PROTECTION

"I lift up my eyes to the mountains—where does my help come from? My help comes from the LORD, the Maker of heaven and earth. He will not let your foot slip—he who watches over you will not slumber; indeed, he who watches over Israel will neither slumber nor sleep."

PSALM 121:1–4

POWER

"Yours, LORD, is the greatness and the power and the glory and the majesty and the splendor, for everything in heaven and earth is yours. Yours, LORD, is the kingdom; you are exalted as head over all."

1 CHRONICLES 29:11

Whatever hit we get from tooting our own horns pales by comparison with the symphony of heaven's praise. When we disengage from the world's way of mattering, then we're free. We're truly free to do whatever God calls us to do. And friend, there is nothing more life-giving and delightful than a heart secure enough to go where he goes, move where he moves.

ALLISON ALLEN

SESSION 3

solo study

Hidden: Finding Delight in Your Life with Christ

Between group sessions, reflect on and dive into the application of the concepts presented in each video across four days.

If there were any group discussion questions your group was unable to get to in your time together, turn back to them and consider them in your personal time as well. Make note of anything you would like to bring up in your next group meeting as you work through this material.

Sink in. See what amazing things unfold. May your time with God be life-giving, productive, and sweet.

solo study

SESSION 3, DAY 1

Truth Statement

God is preparing me for a purpose.

Read

"Commit to the LORD whatever you do, and he will establish your plans. The LORD works out everything to its proper end—even the wicked for a day of disaster."

PROVERBS 16:3–4

Reflect

1. **Why does God long to be involved in your daily life, in "whatever" you do day by day?**

2. **How would your planning process look different if you were to commit "whatever you do" to God?**

Respond

This session's concealed character, Huldah, lived during an especially dark season in history, yet she stayed faithful to God's will and ways. We can't know if she was aware that her faithfulness would one day be rewarded by her being called on to testify to the truth of God's Word, but that's exactly what unfolded. And we know from Proverbs 3:32 that God "detests the perverse but takes the upright into his confidence."

What is one habit you will commit to this week that will help you to stand firm in the light of God's truth despite darkness in the culture at large?

- ☐ Daily Bible reading
- ☐ Praying before checking the phone each morning
- ☐ Practicing gratitude instead of grumbling
- ☐ Prompt confession of sin
- ☐ Something else? ______________________________

Prayer Journal

Consider the prompt below. Complete the sentence as a prayer that reflects your declaration and hope and purpose.

"You are preparing me for . . ."

solo study

SESSION 3, DAY 2

Truth Statement

God protects me eternally.

Read

"So do not fear, for I am with you; do not be dismayed, for I am your God. I will strengthen you and help you; I will uphold you with my righteous right hand."

ISAIAH 41:10

Reflect

1. **What circumstances in your life today warrant God's protecting power, and why?**

2. **How might your perspective on the challenges you're facing shift as you remember that God is strengthening and upholding you even now?**

Respond

In this session's video segment, Allison talked about being influenced by a master gardener, who taught her that even a plant that ultimately needs full sun exposure to thrive must first spend time in the protective covering of shade until its root system is strengthened to withstand the blazing heat.

What "roots" do you hope to drive down deep now, so that when God calls on you to step out into the sunlight, you are strong enough to succeed? Is it the "root" of Bible literacy? The "root" of satisfaction with being seen by God and not by the world? The "root" of familiarity with your heavenly Father through prayer? The "root" of comfort with solitude—being alone in a perfectly still and silent space?

Note your thoughts below.

Prayer Journal

Consider the prompt below. Complete the sentence as a prayer that reflects your gratitude, acknowledgement, and praise.

"Lord, I thank you. You hide me . . ."

solo study

SESSION 3, DAY 3

Truth Statement

The only true power is God's.

Read

"Yours, LORD, is the greatness and the power and the glory and the majesty and the splendor, for everything in heaven and earth is yours. Yours, LORD, is the kingdom; you are exalted as head over all."

1 CHRONICLES 29:11

Reflect

1. **Do you think human beings are meant to possess power? Why, or why not?**

2. **How effectively have you stewarded power throughout your life?**

Respond

Huldah's legacy to this day is that when God shone a spotlight on her life, she showed up boldly and confidently ready to testify to the truth of God's Word. The fact is, King Josiah could have called on well-known prophets of his day such as Zephaniah, but he didn't. He tasked five men with finding Huldah. Why? Because he knew that Huldah could be trusted to tell the truth.

This begs the question, *Are you known as a truth-teller, too?*

If we have the truth of God's Word "in us," then the truth of God's Word is what will come *out of us*, even when the stakes are high. What is one truth from Scripture that you will write on your mind and heart today? Select one from the options below or fill in a verse of your own choosing on the lines that follow.

How might God use this truth you're hiding away to impact his world for good?

- ☐ "The fear of the LORD is the beginning of wisdom, and knowledge of the Holy One is understanding" (Proverbs 9:10).
- ☐ "Peacemakers who sow in peace reap a harvest of righteousness" (James 3:18).
- ☐ "As obedient children, do not conform to the evil desires you had when you lived in ignorance. But just as he who called you is holy, so be holy in all you do; for it is written: 'Be holy, because I am holy'" (1 Peter 1:14–16).
- ☐ "Therefore, as God's chosen people, holy and dearly loved, clothe yourselves with compassion, kindness, humility, gentleness and patience" (Colossians 3:12).
- ☐ "But those who hope in the LORD will renew their strength. They will soar on wings like eagles; they will run and not grow weary, they will walk and not be faint" (Isaiah 40:31).
- ☐ ______________________________

____

____

Prayer Journal

Consider the prompt below. Complete the sentence as a prayer that reflects an honest confession and humble request.

"Lord, in my weakness . . ."

solo study

SESSION 3, DAY 4

Truth Statement

God's timing is perfect.

Read

"Let us not become weary in doing good, for at the proper time we will reap a harvest if we do not give up."

GALATIANS 6:9

Reflect

1. **How do you think God defines what Galatians 6:9 calls "the proper time"?**

2. **When have you benefited from trusting God's timing in your life, even though things unfolded differently than what you had planned?**

Respond

We see in the life of Huldah that "bearing fruit" meant things like being available to serve and minister in the name of God, knowing God's Word so well that when called upon she could affirm what was true, and anchoring herself so deeply in God's strength that she could boldly deliver bad news even when it was risky to do so.

If God came to you and asked what kind of fruit you hoped to bear someday, how would you answer him? What righteous dreams would you dream if you had the presence of mind to do so?

Note your insights below.

Prayer Journal

Consider the prompt below. Complete the sentence as a prayer that reflects a hope of bearing fruit in Christ.

"Jesus, may my life bear fruit . . ."

SESSION 4

what lies beneath the surface of our lives

Believing that All Will Be Revealed

"There is nothing concealed that will not be disclosed, or hidden that will not be made known. What I tell you in the dark, speak in the daylight; what is whispered in your ear, proclaim from the roofs."

MATTHEW 10:26–27

"Hide yourself in my ways . . ."

Session Introduction

15 min.

Ask a group member to read this section aloud as you begin your time together.

If you've ever been to a carnival or circus where funhouse mirrors were part of the scene, then you know that upon peering into them, nothing is as it seems. What's right-side-up looks upside-down. What's normal in size seems dramatically inflated or wildly thin. Through the illusionary contortions of a funhouse mirror, an average-framed child is suddenly twelve feet tall, pencil thin, and the possessor of Mickey Mouse-size hands.

The "fun" part of funhouse mirrors is that our expectations are violated in surprising and humorous ways. We think we will find one thing and are thus shocked when we find another.

The gospel is a lot like this, in that it violates expectations, too.

In various places throughout Scripture, Jesus confirms that while we expect one set of things to be true—in life here on earth and in eternity—in fact, *another* set of things is what we should prepare for, if we are to be considered followers of his. Consider these paradoxes Jesus introduced to his disciples, during his ministry here on earth:

- God exalts the humble and humbles the exalted (1 Peter 5:6).
- We can learn to see unseen things (2 Corinthians 4:18).
- We gain strength by becoming weak (2 Corinthians 13:9).
- To be great, we must serve others (Luke 22:26).
- The first must choose to be last (Matthew 20:16).
- To receive, we voluntarily give (Luke 6:38).
- We only live when we willingly die (Luke 9:23).
- To experience real rest, we take on a yoke—the yoke of Christ (Matthew 11:28–30).
- To become wise, we become fools for Christ's sake (1 Corinthians 3:18–21).

And then there is this paradox, which we will turn to during this session: it's in our sin being revealed—whether to others or to ourselves—that we find freedom because only what is revealed can be divinely healed.

Jesus—both his person and his ways—was considered "strange" by Pilate's wife, this session's concealed character, and for good reason: he *is* strange. His ways *are* strange. And as we'll soon see, this is a very good thing.

A Note on Time and Place: The Customary Release of a Prisoner

Ask a group member to read the following section aloud to get your bearings regarding this session's primary biblical account.

In the ancient world Passover, the celebration honoring the Israelites' exodus from Egypt following four hundred years of slavery, was honored on the fifteenth day of the Hebrew month of Nisan,[1] (on our modern calendar, March or April), which would have always fallen on a full moon.

With Passover came scores of traditions, each one a symbol for some aspect of the holiday's origins: preparedness, freedom, victory, unity, rescue, strength, redemption, hope that brighter days are to come.

They would clean their homes. They would eat unleavened bread and bitter herbs. They would enjoy a special family meal together. They would retell the Passover story from the book of Exodus and sing special songs of praise to God.

And then there was this: they would gather in the central court and in one voice ask the Roman governor to release a single convict, a prisoner—most often a political prisoner—who would have been killed.[2] The Jewish people had differing political views, and this act of solidarity intended to remind them that for one day, anyway, the day of the Passover celebration, they could set aside those differences and honor their shared history.

It is during this release that our concealed character, Pilate's wife, emerges, with a whispered caution on her lips.

Session 4 Concealed Character

> **Ask a group member to read the following Scripture passage aloud, which features this session's "concealed character."**

PILATE'S WIFE

"Meanwhile Jesus stood before the governor, and the governor asked him, 'Are you the king of the Jews?'

'You have said so,' Jesus replied.

When he was accused by the chief priests and the elders, he gave no answer. Then Pilate asked him, 'Don't you hear the testimony they are bringing against you?' But Jesus made no reply, not even to a single charge—to the great amazement of the governor.

Now it was the governor's custom at the festival to release a prisoner chosen by the crowd. At that time they had a well-known prisoner whose name was Jesus Barabbas. So when the crowd had gathered, Pilate asked them, 'Which one do you want me to release to you: Jesus Barabbas, or Jesus who is called the Messiah?' For he knew it was out of self-interest that they had handed Jesus over to him.

While Pilate was sitting on the judge's seat, his wife sent him this message: 'Don't have anything to do with that innocent man, for I have suffered a great deal today in a dream because of him.'

But the chief priests and the elders persuaded the crowd to ask for Barabbas and to have Jesus executed.

'Which of the two do you want me to release to you?' asked the governor.

'Barabbas,' they answered.

'What shall I do, then, with Jesus who is called the Messiah?' Pilate asked.

They all answered, 'Crucify him!'

'Why? What crime has he committed?' asked Pilate.

But they shouted all the louder, 'Crucify him!'

When Pilate saw that he was getting nowhere, but that instead an uproar was starting, he took water and washed his hands in front of the crowd. 'I am innocent of this man's blood,' he said. 'It is your responsibility!'

All the people answered, 'His blood is on us and on our children!'

Then he released Barabbas to them. But he had Jesus flogged, and handed him over to be crucified."

MATTHEW 27:11–26

Group Time

Prepare to Watch: 5 min.

Prior to screening the video segment, spend a few minutes in prayer. The following scripturally supported prayer points deal directly with this session's content, but tailor this time to the distinct needs of the members in your group.

If we are hip-deep in the throes of sinfulness and waywardness, the apostle Paul says that we can, "examine yourselves to see whether you are in the faith" (**2 Corinthians 13:5**). By God's divine power and insight, we can obtain an accurate assessment of how we're living life.

Upon realizing that we have gone astray, we can come before God and claim his forgiveness. "If we confess our sins," **1 John 1:9** promises, "he [God] is faithful and just and will forgive us our sins and purify us from all unrighteousness."

God forgives us for our sin and commits to renovating our lives, as Paul wrote in **Philippians 1:6**: "being confident of this, that he [God] who began a good work in you will carry it on to completion until the day of Christ Jesus."

Play Video Session 4 using streaming code or DVD: 22 min.

Use the space below to log your thoughts or key takeaways from the video teaching.

Red-flag warnings

Beneath life's waterlines

> *"Scripture promises us that there is nothing hidden that will not be revealed."*
>
> ALLISON ALLEN

A woman accustomed to privilege and power

Who will rescue us, indeed?

God's command to Baruch

A look at Baruch's heart

Pride that takes us under

Seeking versus stewarding great things

Discussion Questions: 45 min.

Work through the following questions as a group, choosing the ones that are most useful to your group.

1. **When was the last time you knew you were in need of rescue, whether the predicament was physical in nature like Allison described when her husband was caught in a rip current, or was of another kind—relational, financial, emotional, spiritual, and so forth? What were the circumstances involved, and what unfolded after you made the realization that you needed help?**

   What are your thoughts on the experience now that you have the opportunity to look back on it?

2. **Assign each of the following passages to various group members to look up and read aloud. What do you learn about the kind of life God longs for his children to live?**

Bible Reference	Description of God's Desire for Us
Psalm 5:12	
Psalm 23:1–4	
Proverbs 1:5	
Psalm 1:1–3	
Hebrews 13:18	
Isaiah 1:16–20	

"We know that there can be spiritual rip tides, attitudes, brokenness, and sin patterns that Jesus, our sanctifying Savior, is relentless in diving down deep to reach. Who will free us from ourselves?"

ALLISON ALLEN

3. **In question 1 you reflected on a recent time when you were in need of rescue but surely could note many more that you've faced across the years. Why do you think God casts such lofty visions for our earthly lives when he surely knows how often our firsthand experience will be so vastly different from that idyllic state?**

Ask a group member to read this section aloud before continuing your discussion.

Just as Pilate's wife knew without a doubt that there was something strange about Jesus, something different about his demeanor, something she'd never seen before in the way he dealt with being accused and abused, every person ever to walk the planet is confronted by Christ's distinction.

He *is* strange. He *is* different. He *is* unlike anyone we've ever seen. And just as Pilate's wife faced a point of decision after she encountered Jesus (for even "doing nothing" but advising her husband to distance himself from Jesus was in effect deciding not to surrender to him), you and I must decide how we will respond.

There are only two options upon being faced with the wholeness and holiness of Christ: we can either surrender to his lordship in a posture of humble gratitude, or we can brazenly persist in our sin.

Eventually, though, even those who denied Jesus as Lord will come to the realization that their sin simply can't deliver what it promises to do. It can't satisfy. It can't heal. It can't fill the God-shaped void inside every human heart. It can't lead us to things that exist in God alone: contentment, purpose, peace, hope, joy.

This is why the apostle Paul bemoaned his sin-streaked condition in Romans 7:19–24 (see callout). We do what we don't want to do and neglect to do the things we should! We know better! We know better because we have read the Word of God. We know the only solution to our consistent conundrum is to let our merciful heavenly Father have his compassionate and restorative way.

> "For I do not do the good I want to do, but the evil I do not want to do—this I keep on doing. Now if I do what I do not want to do, it is no longer I who do it, but it is sin living in me that does it.
>
> "So I find this law at work: Although I want to do good, evil is right there with me. For in my inner being I delight in God's law; but I see another law at work in me, waging war against the law of my mind and making me a prisoner of the law of sin at work within me. What a wretched man I am! Who will rescue me from this body that is subject to death?"
>
> —ROMANS 7:19–24

4. **In the video segment, Allison drew our attention to two biblical figures who in their outright denial of God's authority attempted to exert self-made power over him.**

   What correlation do you see between King Jehoiakim throwing the Word of God into the fire (see Jeremiah 36:20–26 to refresh your understanding of the story) and Pilate's wife trying with every fiber of her being to distance her family from Jesus Christ?

5. **We can run from truth like Pilate's wife did. We can even burn the truth, as did King Jehoiakim. But the truth will remain the truth, and there will be an accounting one day for whether we lived like it was true or not.**

   What is one aspect of God's truth that you've been running from lately, an aspect that despite your fervent denial will forever and always be *true*?

6. **What will change in your present reality once you embrace this particular truth?**

"Who will dive beneath the waterlines of our lives and bring order to the forces of the flesh, the world, and the enemy himself? Well, that would be Jesus Christ."

ALLISON ALLEN

Before You Go: 5 min.

Pray as a group through the scriptural truths below from each category. Ask God to help you to communicate one of these truths to someone before your group convenes for session 5.

GOD'S WORD

"For the word of God is alive and active. Sharper than any double-edged sword, it penetrates even to dividing soul and spirit, joints and marrow; it judges the thoughts and attitudes of the heart."

HEBREWS 4:12

PRAYER

"Rejoice always, pray continually, give thanks in all circumstances; for this is God's will for you in Christ Jesus."

1 THESSALONIANS 5:16–18

COMMUNITY

"Carry each other's burdens, and in this way you will fulfill the law of Christ."

GALATIANS 6:2

"Most of us want to know if there is something unseen that threatens to take us down. May we summon the courage to ask Jesus to encounter us in the oceanic trenches of our lives, those deep places where things feel bottomless. The truth is, even in the depth of our sin, Jesus is there, life preserver in hand."

SESSION 4

solo study

Hidden: Finding Delight in Your Life with Christ

Between group sessions, reflect on and dive into the application of the concepts presented in each video across four days.

If there were any group discussion questions your group was unable to get to in your time together, turn back to them and consider them in your personal time as well. Make note of anything you would like to bring up in your next group meeting as you work through this material.

Sink in. See what amazing things unfold. May your time with God be life-giving, productive, and sweet.

solo study

SESSION 4, DAY 1

Truth Statement

In Christ, God accepts me.

Read

"See what great love the Father has lavished on us, that we should be called children of God! And that is what we are! The reason the world does not know us is that it did not know him."

1 JOHN 3:1

Reflect

1. **What difference does it make to your self-concept that as a believer in Christ, God considers you his beloved child?**

2. **We learned in the video segment that God told his scribe Baruch that while he, God, would indeed execute judgment on his nation Israel, he would spare Baruch's life. Why do you think God showed Baruch mercy?**

   What posture do you think your heavenly Father assumes with you whenever you fall short of fulfilling his plans for your life?

Respond

Sometimes it's easier to make sense of God accepting other people who mess up than it is to believe he accepts us, too. But the good news of the gospel affirms that it was *while we were dead in our sin* that God sent his Son, Jesus, to save us (Romans 5:8). In other words, God did for us what we could never do for ourselves: he imparted to us his Son's perfection so that we could come close to God.

Look up Galatians 2:20 in your Bible, write the words of that verse on the lines below, and then answer the questions that follow.

Why do you suppose the apostle Paul said that to be in a surrendered relationship with Christ necessitates dying to self?

Why should believers find this necessity a *very good thing*?

Prayer Journal

Consider the prompt below. Complete the sentence as a prayer that reflects an acknowledgement for all the ways you are known to God and how.

"Lord, you love me . . ."

solo study

SESSION 4, DAY 2

Truth Statement

God examines me.

Read

"Though you probe my heart,
    though you examine me at night and test me,
you will find that I have planned no evil;
    my mouth has not transgressed."

PSALM 17:3

Reflect

1. **What is the primary emotion you experience when you read the psalmist's words regarding God coming at night to "examine" the hearts of those who say they love him? What experiences or assumptions shape your response?**

2. **What qualities do you believe qualify God for performing such "examinations" on his children?**

Respond

If God were to come to you tonight as you were falling asleep, perform a "heart examination" on you as the psalmist described, and find your heart free from deception in all its forms, what things would you need to confess to him now, to clear the air between him and you?

Consider closing your time today with several minutes of unhurried, silent prayer. Claim the forgiveness your Father longs to extend to you now. He is waiting with grace in hand.

Prayer Journal

Consider the prompt below. Complete the sentence as a prayer that reflects yourself as a humble offering.

"As you examine me, Father, may you be pleased with . . ."

solo study

SESSION 4, DAY 3

Truth Statement

God tells me the truth.

Read

"The LORD detests dishonest scales, but accurate weights find favor with him."

PROVERBS 11:1

Reflect

1. **When have you encountered God's truth afresh and chosen to make a change in your life to align with it? What were the circumstances, what was the bit of truth you bumped up against, and what happened as a result of your taking a fresh step of surrender toward God?**

"The problem is not in stewarding great things, but in seeking them. Have I confused stewarding the great things God does with seeking great things for myself?"

ALLISON ALLEN

2. **What does it mean to you that whenever you want to know the truth about how you're doing in life, you can come to God, you can hear from God, and you can be supernaturally empowered to course-correct then and there?**

Respond

In this session's video segment, Allison explained that while the pride that festered inside Baruch's heart was unseen by those who knew and loved him, it was not unseen by God. God always sees the truth of our lives, and he is always willing to share that truth with us.[1]

In the time that remains, read through the following prompts, asking God to shoot straight with you and listen for how to respond.

God, what do you see when you look at my closest relationships these days?

How can I be more careful with the words that I speak?

How am I faithfully telling people about my relationship with you?

In what ways have I become prideful during this season of life?

What habit or lifestyle pattern of mine is upsetting to you?

What sin have I failed to confess?

Prayer Journal

Consider the prompt below. Complete the sentence as a prayer that reflects your committed trust in the Lord.

"God, I can trust you. I can trust your every word to . . ."

solo study

SESSION 4, DAY 4

Truth Statement

God works for my good.

Read

"And we know that in all things God works for the good of those who love him, who have been called according to his purpose."

ROMANS 8:28

Reflect

1. **What has it looked like during previous seasons of your life for God to work "for the good" on your behalf?**

2. **How would you describe your level of faith that God will continue to work for your good during the days to come?**

Respond

During the video segment Allison told the story of her husband being trapped by a rip current, requiring two lifeguards to risk their own safety to lead him back to shore. She said of her husband, "He remembers being exhausted from trying to stay afloat and finally surrendering to the lifeguards' strength."

What would it look like, given your present circumstances, to quit paddling so hard to try in vain to stay afloat, to surrender to your heavenly Father's strength, and to be led back to the path of righteousness that God longs for you to tread?

Prayer Journal

Consider the prompt below. Complete the sentence as a prayer that reflects your faith in the Lord in all things.

"Lord, I believe in all things you are . . ."

SESSION 5

out of hiding

Getting Unstuck to Serve God

"When Jesus spoke again to the people, he said, 'I am the light of the world. Whoever follows me will never walk in darkness, but will have the light of life.'"

JOHN 8:12

"Hide yourself in my will . . ."

Session Introduction

15 min.

Ask a group member to read this section aloud as you begin your time together.

Have you ever noticed how overwhelming life can sometimes seem? There are mouths to feed. Spaces to clean. Prayers to pray. Tasks to check off. Errands to run. Projects to complete. Plans to be made. Laundry to fold. Always, *always* laundry to fold. And this says nothing of the days when sickness comes, or when the check *doesn't* come, or when the news is grim, or when the bottom just totally falls out.

It takes a lot to keep things moving forward . . . a lot of time, a lot of energy, a lot of patience, a lot of *sorting things out*. And for most of us on those days, it feels like a grand accomplishment to reach bedtime with everyone still alive and relatively happy.

Which is why it can feel like a cruel taunt to learn that as believers, in addition to managing our daily lives, God expects us to *also* help accomplish what's on *his* celestial to-do list. You know it as the Great Commission, his plea to his followers to "go and make disciples of all nations, baptizing them in the name of the Father and of the Son and of the Holy Spirit, and teaching them to obey everything I have commanded you. And surely I am with you always, to the very end of the age" (Matthew 28:19–20).

To which many believers are tempted to say, "Wait, what? *When*?" Doesn't God know that we have our hands full already? And that talking to people about spiritual things makes us anxious? And that we'd rather stay home on the couch?

Praise God for his patience with us. His compassion toward us. His patience whenever we've lost the plot. "It's okay, child," he says with tenderness to spare. "I'll go with you. We've got this. We've got this because I've got you."

He knows that what makes life meaningful is living it in Christ, with Christ, and for Christ. And so he gives us strength to do just that.

A Note on Time and Place: The Ancient Winepress

Ask a group member to read the following section aloud to get your bearings regarding this session's primary biblical account.

In this session's key biblical passage, we find the judge and prophet Gideon threshing wheat in a winepress when an angel of the Lord appears to him with an invitation to join God in his redemptive work.

In those days, lacking the machinery of our current age, wheat would be separated from chaff on an outdoor threshing floor. After the wheat was tossed into the air, allowing the airy chaff to be carried on the wind, the heavier grain would fall to the floor, where workers would manually pick off the dirt and other impurities that still clung to the pieces of wheat.[1]

In Gideon's case, however, the threshing couldn't occur in such a visible place. We learn from the text that because Gideon needed to conceal his work from the Midianites, who were known to come into Israel and destroy their crops and thus their livelihood, he was relegated to threshing in an underground winepress. It was here in something of a constricted stone well that God's angel paid him a visit, to make him an offer: come join God in the wide-open space where he works.

Session 5 Concealed Character

Ask a group member to read the following Scripture passage aloud, which features this session's "concealed character."

GIDEON, ISRAELI JUDGE AND PROPHET

"The angel of the LORD came and sat down under the oak in Ophrah that belonged to Joash the Abiezrite, where his son Gideon was threshing wheat in a winepress to keep it from the Midianites. When the angel of the LORD appeared to Gideon, he said, 'The LORD is with you, mighty warrior.'

'Pardon me, my lord,' Gideon replied, 'but if the LORD is with us, why has all this happened to us? Where are all his wonders that our ancestors told us about when they said, "Did not the LORD bring us up out of Egypt?" But now the LORD has abandoned us and given us into the hand of Midian.'

The LORD turned to him and said, 'Go in the strength you have and save Israel out of Midian's hand. Am I not sending you?'

'Pardon me, my lord,' Gideon replied, 'but how can I save Israel? My clan is the weakest in Manasseh, and I am the least in my family.'

The LORD answered, 'I will be with you, and you will strike down all the Midianites, leaving none alive.'

Gideon replied, 'If now I have found favor in your eyes, give me a sign that it is really you talking to me. Please do not go away until I come back and bring my offering and set it before you.'

And the LORD said, 'I will wait until you return.'

Gideon went inside, prepared a young goat, and from an ephah of flour he made bread without yeast. Putting the meat in a basket and its broth in a pot, he brought them out and offered them to him under the oak.

The angel of God said to him, 'Take the meat and the unleavened bread, place them on this rock, and pour out the broth.' And Gideon did so. Then the angel of the LORD touched the meat and the unleavened bread with the tip of the staff that was in his hand. Fire flared from the rock, consuming the meat and the bread. And the angel of the LORD disappeared. When Gideon realized that it was the angel of the LORD, he exclaimed, 'Alas, Sovereign LORD! I have seen the angel of the LORD face to face!'

But the LORD said to him, 'Peace! Do not be afraid. You are not going to die.'

So Gideon built an altar to the LORD there and called it The LORD Is Peace. To this day it stands in Ophrah of the Abiezrites."

JUDGES 6:11–24

Group Time

Prepare to Watch: 5 min.

Prior to screening the video segment, spend a few minutes in prayer. The following biblically supported prayer points deal directly with this session's content, but tailor this time to the distinct needs of the members in your group.

We can become consumed by our own work, our own goals, our own to-do's, even as God is at work all around us. In **John 4:34**, we are reminded that Jesus viewed God's work as the only necessary work: "My food," he said, "is to do the will of him who sent me and to finish his work."

God longs for us to join him in his work according to **Ephesians 2:10**, which says, that we are "God's handiwork, created in Christ Jesus to do good works, which God prepared in advance for us to do."

We need so little faith to accomplish the will of God! **Luke 17:6** reminds us of this truth from Jesus: "If you have faith as small as a mustard seed, you can say to this mulberry tree, 'Be uprooted and planted in the sea,' and it will obey you.'"

True satisfaction and sturdiness in life come from partnering with God. "As for everyone who comes to me and hears my words and puts them into practice," Jesus said in **Luke 6:46–48**, "I will show you what they are like. They are like a man building a house, who dug down deep and laid the foundation on rock. When a flood came, the torrent struck that house but could not shake it, because it was well built."

Play Video Session 5 using streaming code or DVD: 19 min.

Use the space below to log your thoughts or key takeaways from the video teaching.

The usefulness of lighthouses

Gideon's story

"Being hidden with Christ in God is an invitation from God, and it's a beautiful, glorious spiritual reality. But hiding? Now, that's a human bent. A reaction to myriad things: pain, fear, insecurity, overexposure. In an emotional and spiritual sense, too often we confuse one with the other."

ALLISON ALLEN

When hiddenness becomes hiding

Asking God to "grace" our go

A body in motion

"When I am stuck in a place of hiding, my heart is transformed by moving, not by staying still."

ALLISON ALLEN

Go in the strength you don't yet know you have

Strength in our weakness

Already safe, already secure

Discussion Questions: 45 min.

> Work through the following questions as a group, choosing the ones that are most useful to your group.

1. In this session's key Bible passage, we see Gideon making a litany of excuses as to why he surely isn't the right guy for God to use in completing such an important mission. Can you relate? When have you *but-but-but-ed* a request God was making of you? What were the circumstances involved, how did you respond, and what transpired from there?

2. Why do you think God chooses to use frail and fallible human beings to achieve his work in the world? He is *God*. He needs nothing to accomplish his will.

"God has chosen what is weak in the world to shame the strong. God has chosen what is insignificant and despised in the world, what is viewed as nothing, to bring to nothing what is viewed as something, so that no one may boast in his presence."

ALLISON ALLEN

3. What fears or insecurities rise to the surface for you whenever God prompts you to say something or to fall silent, to do something or to purposefully abstain from taking action you desperately want to take?

Ask a group member to read this section aloud before continuing your discussion.

Perhaps it's a good thing that for most people the response to being summoned by God to participate in his work is one of shrinking back, making excuses, and scanning the room for the quickest way out. After all, God is *other.* He is *beyond.* We learn from an Old Testament prophet that God's thoughts are not our thoughts, and his ways are not our ways (see Isaiah 55:8). It's natural that we would look upon a direct invitation from the Almighty with more than a hint of suspicion. *Are you sure you're talking to . . . me?*

That same prophet, the prophet Isaiah, upon being commissioned by God to warn his people of impending judgment, experienced this very thing. You may recall the scene from Isaiah 6, which reads: "In the year that King Uzziah died, I saw the Lord, high and exalted, seated on a throne; and the train of his robe filled the temple. Above him were seraphim, each with six wings: With two wings they covered their faces, with two they covered their feet, and with two they were flying. And they were calling to one another: 'Holy, holy, holy is the LORD Almighty; the whole earth is full of his glory.'

"At the sound of their voices the doorposts and thresholds shook and the temple was filled with smoke. 'Woe to me!' I cried. 'I am ruined! For I am a man of unclean lips, and I live among a people of unclean lips, and my eyes have seen the King, the LORD Almighty.'

"Then one of the seraphim flew to me with a live coal in his hand, which he had taken with tongs from the altar. With it he touched my mouth and said, 'See, this has touched your lips; your guilt is taken away and your sin atoned for.'

"Then I heard the voice of the Lord saying, 'Whom shall I send? And who will go for us?'

"And I said, 'Here I am. Send me!'" (verses 1–8).

The lesson we learn from Isaiah's experience: It's okay to recognize God's *otherness.* It's okay to be in awe. It's even okay to question our worthiness to do what God's asking us to do. But ultimately, we've got to go.

Ultimately, God warrants a *yes.*

4. **During the video segment, Allison said that when the angel told Gideon to "go in the strength you have," what he likely meant was, "go in the strength you *don't yet know*." Can you relate? When have you experienced an infusion of divine strength that you didn't believe you possessed? What was the situation, and why did you need the boost? What happened as a result?**

   Who got the glory in the end?

5. **What keeps you from stepping out in faith more often these days? Which dynamic tends to cause your otherwise "ready yes" to hitch in your throat?**

   Select one of the options Allison mentioned during the video segment, or add one to the list that is truer of your experience:

   - ☐ Humility that has slid into **self-humiliation**: I'm not up to the task. I'm not the right person. I'm not qualified, God! There's bound to be someone else.
   - ☐ Discernment that has slid into **criticism**: The person you want me to help isn't worthy of my time and attention. This is beneath me. I don't have bandwidth for this.
   - ☐ Mercy that has slid into **enabling**: If I do what you're asking me to do, things will fall apart. They need me. They need my help. I have to keep doing what I'm doing.
   - ☐ Hiddenness that has slid into **hiding** from God: Don't make me do this, God. I don't want to get up. I don't want to do this. I don't want to be part of it. I just don't want to go.

☐ ____________________

6. **In Judges 8 (see callout), we read of what resulted from Gideon's participation in God's work following the defeat of the Midianite forces. Ask someone in your group to read the verses aloud and then answer the three questions below.**

> "The Israelites said to Gideon, 'Rule over us—you, your son and your grandson—because you have saved us from the hand of Midian.'
>
> "But Gideon told them, 'I will not rule over you, nor will my son rule over you. The Lord will rule over you.' And he said, 'I do have one request, that each of you give me an earring from your share of the plunder.' (It was the custom of the Ishmaelites to wear gold earrings.)
>
> "They answered, 'We'll be glad to give them.' So they spread out a garment, and each of them threw a ring from his plunder onto it. The weight of the gold rings he asked for came to seventeen hundred shekels, not counting the ornaments, the pendants and the purple garments worn by the kings of Midian or the chains that were on their camels' necks.
>
> "Gideon made the gold into an ephod, which he placed in Ophrah, his town. All Israel prostituted themselves by worshiping it there, and it became a snare to Gideon and his family.
>
> "Thus Midian was subdued before the Israelites and did not raise its head again. During Gideon's lifetime, the land had peace forty years.
>
> "Jerub-Baal son of Joash went back home to live. He had seventy sons of his own, for he had many wives. His concubine, who lived in Shechem, also bore him a son, whom he named Abimelek. Gideon son of Joash died at a good old age and was buried in the tomb of his father Joash in Ophrah of the Abiezrites.
>
> "No sooner had Gideon died than the Israelites again prostituted

themselves to the Baals. They set up Baal-Berith as their god and did not remember the Lord their God, who had rescued them from the hands of all their enemies on every side. They also failed to show any loyalty to the family of Jerub-Baal (that is, Gideon) in spite of all the good things he had done for them."

—JUDGES 8:22–35

Why do you think Gideon was compelled to clarify that it would be God and not him leading the people going forward?

What do you make of the fact that despite Gideon's noble investment in kingdom work, immediately following his death the people went right back to sinning against God?

Do you think it's worth it to join God in his work when fruitfulness from those efforts isn't guaranteed?

Before You Go: 5 min.

Pray as a group through the scriptural truths below from each category. Ask God to help you to communicate one of these truths to someone before your group convenes for session 6.

FRIENDSHIP WITH GOD

"Greater love has no one than this: to lay down one's life for one's friends. You are my friends if you do what I command. I no longer call you servants, because a servant does not know his master's business. Instead, I have called you friends, for everything that I learned from my Father I have made known to you."

JOHN 15:13–15

FAITHFULNESS TO GOD

"But be sure to fear the LORD and serve him faithfully with all your heart; consider what great things he has done for you."

1 SAMUEL 12:24

FULFILLMENT IN GOD

"The LORD will guide you always; he will satisfy your needs in a sun-scorched land and will strengthen your frame. You will be like a well-watered garden, like a spring whose waters never fail."

ISAIAH 58:11

"Gently reinvest yourself in the truth that you are hidden with Christ in God, no matter what enemy or terror of the enemy threatens to undo in you. The most essential part of who you are, if you've already trusted Christ for salvation, is already safe, already secure, already covered in him."

ALLISON ALLEN

SESSION 5

solo study

Hidden: Finding Delight in Your Life with Christ

Between group sessions, reflect on and dive into the application of the concepts presented in each video across four days.

If there were any group discussion questions your group was unable to get to in your time together, turn back to them and consider them in your personal time as well. Make note of anything you would like to bring up in your next group meeting as you work through this material.

Sink in. See what amazing things unfold. May your time with God be life-giving, productive, and sweet.

solo study

SESSION 5, DAY 1

Truth Statement

God is looking for me.

Read

"They will be called the Holy People, the Redeemed of the LORD;
and you will be called Sought After, the City No Longer Deserted."

ISAIAH 62:12

Reflect

1. **In a day when online "connectedness" is at an all-time high and loneliness is reported as having reached epidemic levels,[1] why is it important that God refers to his children by the name Sought After?**

2. **What would it look like for you to prioritize in your daily life staying "findable" by God?**

Respond

A very real temptation in our digital age is letting the wild sense of control over life that our phones and other devices afford us seep into expectations of our spiritual lives. But regarding our interactions with God, we tap "do not disturb" at our own peril.

He longs to connect with us. He has plans for us. He comes bearing good gifts for us. He hopes that we will engage with him.

Put down your phone—that's the invitation today. You decide when and for how long. What matters is that you do it. That you sit undistracted before your Father with no agenda, no aim.

For today—and maybe tomorrow, too—be findable by God.

Prayer Journal

Consider the prompt below. Complete the sentence as a prayer that reflects your understanding of, or desire to understand, Christ's presence in your life every day.

"I welcome your presence, Lord, which . . ."

solo study

SESSION 5, DAY 2

Truth Statement

God is patient with me.

Read

"Come near to God and he will come near to you . . ."

JAMES 4:8

Reflect

1. How is it possible to experience nearness with a God who cannot be seen?

2. What have you learned along the way from time spent "near" to God?

Respond

Yesterday the goal was simply to be findable by God. Today, the goal is to meet his gaze. Perhaps you'll do this by closing your eyes in prayer. You might sit before a vista and gaze upon creation's beauty. You might choose to read a beloved passage of Scripture several times through.

However you choose to do so, decide to turn toward God today, logging any insights you pick up in the space below.

Prayer Journal

Consider the prompt below. Complete the sentence as a prayer asking God near.

"Lord, come near to me so that . . ."

solo study

SESSION 5, DAY 3

Truth Statement

God emboldens me.

Read

"When I called, you answered me; you greatly emboldened me."

PSALM 138:3

Reflect

1. **What do you think it means for God to "embolden" a person?**

2. **Where do you need a little boost of boldness today?**

Respond

Sit in the presence of God for several minutes, asking him to help you see what he is asking you to do. Who does he want you to forgive? Who does he want you to reach out to or to pray for? What step of faith is he hoping you will take?

Jot down any promptings below that come to mind.

Prayer Journal

Consider the prompt below. Complete the sentence as a prayer that reflects your confidence in Christ.

"I can accomplish what you ask of me because . . ."

solo study

SESSION 5, DAY 4

Truth Statement

God is asking me to go.

Read

"All this is from God, who reconciled us to himself through Christ and gave us the ministry of reconciliation: that God was reconciling the world to himself in Christ, not counting people's sins against them. And he has committed to us the message of reconciliation.

"We are therefore Christ's ambassadors, as though God were making his appeal through us. We implore you on Christ's behalf: Be reconciled to God."

2 CORINTHIANS 5:18–20

Reflect

1. **How might your self-concept be different if the first identity you claimed in your day-to-day life were that of *Christ's ambassador*?**

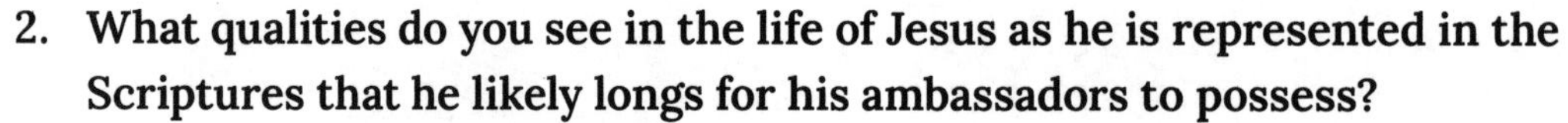

2. **What qualities do you see in the life of Jesus as he is represented in the Scriptures that he likely longs for his ambassadors to possess?**

Respond

Looking back at yesterday's entry, by God's power and encouragement, which of the insights you jotted down are you willing to accomplish today?

Today, *go.*

Do the thing God is asking you to do.

Prayer Journal

Consider the prompt below. Complete the sentence as a prayer that reflects your understanding of God calling you to serve him.

"You are calling me to . . ."

SESSION 6

from strength to strength

Living with a Contented Soul

"Be very careful, then, how you live—not as unwise but as wise, making the most of every opportunity, because the days are evil. Therefore do not be foolish, but understand what the Lord's will is. Do not get drunk on wine, which leads to debauchery. Instead, be filled with the Spirit, speaking to one another with psalms, hymns, and songs from the Spirit. Sing and make music from your heart to the Lord, always giving thanks to God the Father for everything, in the name of our Lord Jesus Christ."

EPHESIANS 5:15–20

"Hide yourself in my worth . . ."

Session Introduction

15 min.

Ask a group member to read this section aloud as you begin your time together.

When was the last time you felt totally and completely content? Were you lakeside taking in a sunset that erupted in oranges and yellows and reds? Was it when your spine relaxed against your mattress after a long and complex day? Maybe it was while you watched your kid walk across the stage on graduation day. Or upon learning that the health scare you'd been dealing with suddenly wasn't so scary after all.

The thing about these episodes of contentment is that they're just that—episodes. They come and go. They begin and end. They're here! And then they're gone, whisps of wind that can't be contained.

What God promises to his children is far different from this. When we live life on God's terms, we know a form of contentment that is not fleeting but enduring, not episodic but persistent, not flighty but deeply rooted in our souls.[1]

This is why the ancient Israelites were compelled to praise God in the course of their daily lives. They knew that despite the challenges they faced and the question marks that plagued them, they could rest in the sure, strong grip of their Lord.

A Note on Time and Place: Solomon's Temple

Ask a group member to read the following section aloud to get your bearings regarding this session's primary biblical account.

Before the Book of Psalms was the series of 150 Bible passages we know and love today, it was a veritable hymnal of choruses the people of Israel sang as they made their way to or from battle, into or out of exile, and, most commonly, back and forth from the Temple in Jerusalem pictured here, where they would gather to worship God.[2]

So many of the psalms are songs of pilgrimage, as Allison notes in this session, rhythmic reminders of God's character, God's promises, and God's redemptive activity throughout the earth.

This session's key text, Psalm 84, was the first of six psalms whose purpose was providing *hope* to the Hebrew people as they looked to God for their future. It delivers hope to readers still today.

Session 6 Concealed Character

Ask a group member to read the following Scripture passage aloud, which features this session's "concealed characters."

THE SONS OF KORAH, PSALMISTS

"How lovely is your dwelling place, LORD Almighty! My soul yearns, even faints, for the courts of the LORD; my heart and my flesh cry out for the living God. Even the sparrow has found a home, and the swallow a nest for herself, where she may have her young—a place near your altar, LORD Almighty, my King and my God.

Blessed are those who dwell in your house; they are ever praising you. Blessed are those whose strength is in you, whose hearts are set on pilgrimage. As they pass through the Valley of Baka, they make it a place of springs; the autumn rains also cover it with pools.

They go from strength to strength, till each appears before God in Zion. Hear my prayer, LORD God Almighty; listen to me, God of Jacob. Look on our shield, O God; look with favor on your anointed one. Better is one day in your courts than a thousand elsewhere; I would rather be a doorkeeper in the house of my God than dwell in the tents of the wicked. For the LORD God is a sun and shield; the LORD bestows favor and honor; no good thing does he withhold from those whose walk is blameless. LORD Almighty, blessed is the one who trusts in you."

PSALM 84

Group Time

Prepare to Watch: 5 min.

Prior to screening the video segment, spend a few minutes in prayer. The following biblically supported prayer points deal directly with this session's content, but tailor this time to the distinct needs of the members in your group.

God is as close as our next breath, lingering here with us. "Where can I go from your Spirit?" the psalmist writes in Psalm 139:7. "Where can I flee from your presence?"

When we turn toward God, acknowledging his presence, we are invited to approach his "throne of grace with confidence, so that we may receive mercy and find grace to help us in our time of need" (Hebrews 4:16).

God longs for us to "enter his gates with thanksgiving and his courts with praise" (Psalm 100:4). Verse 5 continues, "For the Lord is good and his love endures forever; his faithfulness continues through all generations."

The more that we engage with God, the more contentment we will know. In Psalm 131:2, we see the results of encountering God: "But I have calmed and quieted myself," the psalmist writes, "I am like a weaned child with its mother; like a weaned child I am content."

Play Video Session 6 using streaming code or DVD: 22 min.

Use the space below to log your thoughts or key takeaways from the video teaching.

Sea glass

A hymnal of sorts

"When you have run out of words for what you're facing, I promise you someone in the psalms is singing them for you."

ALLISON ALLEN

The sons of Korah

Fully satisfied in God

"No matter the stage or season, visible or invisible, how this world regards or disregards us doesn't matter because we're fully satisfied and satiated in him. God has the final say on our lives, and that sets us free to live secure."

ALLISON ALLEN

A word on Kohath

The day the earth opened up

Contentment is portable

Nesting birds

Discussion Questions: 45 min.

Work through the following questions as a group, choosing the ones that are most useful to your group.

1. **Which part of this session's video segment was most meaningful to you and why?**

2. **What thoughts, emotions, memories, or ideas come to mind as you envision the doves perched on the Western Wall in Israel that Allison mentioned, which is known as the most religious site for the Jewish people and the last remaining wall of the ancient Jewish temple? What situations or experiences in your life tend to prompt you to long to be that close to God?**

3. **What do you suppose the psalmist wanted lovers of God to glean from the reminder in Psalm 84 that "even the sparrow has found a home" in his presence "and the swallow a nest for herself, where she may have her young" (Psalm 84:3)?**

Ask a group member to read this section aloud before continuing your discussion.

We get the sense from the scene Allison referenced involving the birds perched atop the Western Wall that those feathered friends felt totally *at home* there, that this was just where they hung out. This was their daily pattern, coming to that wall, resting on its strength, communing with one another, singing like they had no care in the world.

You can tell a lot about birds—and people too, for that matter—by where they most naturally feel at home.

4. If God has so clearly promised us things like safety and security and sturdiness to move through this life successfully, why do you think more followers of Christ don't experience safety, security, sturdiness, and success with greater regularity?

"Contentment is portable, no matter the role or assignment."

ALLISON ALLEN

5. What do you suppose is the cascading effect in a person's life of pre-deciding each morning to be content throughout that day? Which part of this cascade do you most covet for yourself?

6. What would you hope to gain from increased intimacy with Jesus Christ, and why?

Before You Go: 5 min.

Pray as a group through the scriptural truths below from each category. During your conversation with God, thank him for the truths of the Scriptures you chose. Ask him to help to communicate one of these truths to someone this week.

PROXIMITY

> "The Lord is near to all who call on him, to all who call on him in truth."
>
> **PSALM 145:18**

PILGRIMAGE

> "Walk in obedience to all that the Lord your God has commanded you, so that you may live and prosper and prolong your days in the land that you will possess."
>
> **DEUTERONOMY 5:33**

PRAISE

> "Through Jesus, therefore, let us continually offer to God a sacrifice of praise—the fruit of lips that openly profess his name."
>
> **HEBREWS 13:15**

"No matter what, you are not outside your Father's care. You have an invitation to come in close and to build your nest near the Father's altar, which prefigures the sacrifice of Jesus. Your Father says that you get this best seat in the house of God's goodness because the price has been paid by his Son. We have received this invitation into intimacy with God because we are covered, once and for all."

ALLISON ALLEN

SESSION 6

solo study

Hidden: Finding Delight in Your Life with Christ

Between group sessions, reflect on and dive into the application of the concepts presented in each video across four days.

If there were any group discussion questions your group was unable to get to in your time together, turn back to them and consider them in your personal time as well. Make note of anything you would like to bring up in your next group meeting as you work through this material.

Sink in. See what amazing things unfold. May your time with God be life-giving, productive, and sweet.

solo study

SESSION 6, DAY 1

Truth Statement

God doesn't need me to perform.

Read

"Listen, my people, and I will speak; I will testify against you, Israel: I am God, your God.

I bring no charges against you concerning your sacrifices or concerning your burnt offerings, which are ever before me. I have no need of a bull from your stall or of goats from your pens, for every animal of the forest is mine, and the cattle on a thousand hills.

"I know every bird in the mountains, and the insects in the fields are mine. If I were hungry I would not tell you, for the world is mine, and all that is in it. Do I eat the flesh of bulls or drink the blood of goats?

"Sacrifice thank offerings to God, fulfill your vows to the Most High, and call on me in the day of trouble; I will deliver you, and you will honor me."

PSALM 50:7–15

Reflect

1. **Based on these verses, what do you notice about God's participation in his relationship to his people?**

2. **According to this psalm, what are the two things God *does* want from us? How faithfully do you practice these two actions in your everyday life? What might be the effect of increasing your devotedness to each?**

Respond

Spend a few minutes meditating on your responses to the two questions above. In the space below, jot down a few "non-performative" ways that you can love God today.

Prayer Journal

Consider the prompt below. Complete the sentence as a prayer that recounts rest in Christ.

"I don't have to perform for you or impress you. I can rest in you, Lord, because . . ."

solo study

SESSION 6, DAY 2

Truth Statement

My visibility doesn't determine my value.

Read

"For physical training is of some value, but godliness has value for all things, holding promise for both the present life and the life to come. This is a trustworthy saying that deserves full acceptance.

"That is why we labor and strive, because we have put our hope in the living God, who is the Savior of all people, and especially of those who believe."

1 TIMOTHY 4:8–10

Reflect

1. **As you survey your life to date, would you say you have put more energy into your physical training or into your spiritual training? Are you pleased with your pattern thus far? Why, or why not?**

2. **What is the key distinction made in the first part of this passage that explains why we are wise to focus more on our spiritual development than on our physical development?**

Respond

What descriptors would you use in defining how a "spiritually developed" follower of Jesus thinks, looks, sounds, and acts? Note your insights below.

Prayer Journal

Consider the prompt below. Complete the sentence as a prayer that reflects your surrender to being seen by God alone.

"Lord, you see me, I . . ."

solo study

SESSION 6, DAY 3

Truth Statement

I face a glorious future.

Read

"But we have this treasure in jars of clay to show that this all-surpassing power is from God and not from us. We are hard pressed on every side, but not crushed; perplexed, but not in despair; persecuted, but not abandoned; struck down, but not destroyed.

"We always carry around in our body the death of Jesus, so that the life of Jesus may also be revealed in our body. For we who are alive are always being given over to death for Jesus' sake, so that his life may also be revealed in our mortal body. So then, death is at work in us, but life is at work in you.

"It is written: 'I believed; therefore I have spoken.' Since we have that same spirit of faith, we also believe and therefore speak, because we know that the one who raised the Lord Jesus from the dead will also raise us with Jesus and present us with you to himself. All this is for your benefit, so that the grace that is reaching more and more people may cause thanksgiving to overflow to the glory of God.

"Therefore we do not lose heart. Though outwardly we are wasting away, yet inwardly we are being renewed day by day. For our light and momentary troubles are achieving for us an eternal glory that far outweighs them all. So we fix our eyes not on what is seen, but on what is unseen, since what is seen is temporary, but what is unseen is eternal."

2 CORINTHIANS 4:7–18

Reflect

1. According to this passage, how is it possible for us not to "lose heart"?

2. What circumstances typically cause you to lose heart? What truth from this passage can come to your rescue the next time you are tempted to lose heart?

Respond

What are three ways you can raise your gaze from what this passage says that in context are "light and momentary troubles" and fix your eyes on the unseen today?

Prayer Journal

Consider the prompt below. Complete the sentence that reflects your understanding of the greatness and majesty of God in your life.

"Lord, my troubles are light, . . ."

solo study

SESSION 6, DAY 4

Truth Statement

My delight comes only from God.

Read

"Open my eyes that I may see wonderful things in your law. I am a stranger on earth; do not hide your commands from me. My soul is consumed with longing for your laws at all times. You rebuke the arrogant, who are accursed, those who stray from your commands.

"Remove from me their scorn and contempt, for I keep your statutes. Though rulers sit together and slander me, your servant will meditate on your decrees. Your statutes are my delight; they are my counselors."

PSALM 119:18–24

Reflect

1. **In a given day, what would you say you spend most of your time "meditating" on, or thinking intently about?**

2. **What do you think the correlation is between meditating on God's ways and finding his ways "delightful"?**

Respond

If you were to log the things about God's will and ways that you find "wonderful," what ten things would top that list? Note your insights below.

Prayer Journal

Consider the prompt below. Complete the sentence as a prayer that reflects your heart of gratitude for God's keeping you and covering you.

"I delight in you, God! . . ."

"I pray you've allowed Jesus to release the pressure valve of performance and the driving need to be seen by the world or others, beginning to believe to the core that visibility or lack thereof can never, ever determine your value. That there is a God who sees you in every season. I pray you've been encouraged to look chin up, becoming more heavenly minded, leaning into the glorious freedom that is the life as Colossians says, hidden with Christ in God. I hope you've come to understand the difference between hiding and being hidden, and that hiddenness never equals inactivity. I hope you know that you are never hidden from God, but in God—in his work and in his ultimate win. In his Word and then in his ways. In his will and in his worth, his worth that is transferred through Christ to you. And I hope this knowledge grants you the courage to walk into the glorious future, free to fix your eyes, your mind, your heart on him."

Allison

notes

Session 1

1. For more on these events, see 2 Kings 25.
2. Mervin Breneman, *Ezra, Nehemiah, Esther*, electronic ed., vol. 10, The New American Commentary (Nashville: Broadman & Holman Publishers, 1993), 189, we find this entry: "'Shallum,' as was Rephaiah in v. 9, was ruler of part of the countryside around Jerusalem. Some understand *bĕnôt*, 'daughters,' as 'small towns' and translate 'he and men from small towns.' It is true that *bĕnôt* is used of 'daughter' towns, but here the masculine suffix argues for the NIV translation. If Shallum had no sons, his daughters would have inherited his property (Num 27:1–11). This mention of women involved in the work again demonstrates the extent of Nehemiah's support and his mobilization of the people."
3. For a detailed account of women's status during the late Roman Republic and days of the early empire, see Bruce W. Winter's excellent work, *Roman Wives, Roman Widows: The Appearance of New Women and the Pauline Communities* (Grand Rapids, MI: Eerdmans, 2003).

Session 1 Solo Study

1. *Strong's Concise Dictionary of the Words of the Hebrew Bible and the Greek Testament*, 6754. צֶלֶם *tselem, tseh´-lem*; from an unused root mean to shade; a phantom, i.e. (fig.) illusion, resemblance; hence a representative figure, espec. an idol:—image, vain shew.
2. James Strong, A *Concise Dictionary of the Words in the Greek Testament and The Hebrew Bible* (Bellingham, WA: Logos Bible Software, 2009), 99.

Session 2

1. From *Dictionary of the Later New Testament & Its Developments*: "Syncretism is the incorporation into religious faith and practice of elements from other religions, resulting in a loss of integrity and assimilation to the surrounding culture."

2. From Thomas V. Brisco's entry in *Holman Bible Atlas*, Holman Reference (Nashville, TN: Broadman & Holman Publishers, 1998), 29:

> "Major religious festivals marked key events in the agricultural year. The Old Testament commanded attendance at three great pilgrim festivals, all of which originally possessed agricultural or pastoral significance (Exod. 23:14–17; Deut. 16:13–17). Passover with its companion Feast of Unleavened Bread not only commemorated the Exodus from Egypt but also marked the beginning of the barley and wheat harvest. The Feast of Weeks, or Firstfruits (Pentecost), celebrated seven weeks after Passover, culminated the cereal harvesttime. Later, in the fall, the Feast of Ingathering, or Booths (Tabernacles), perhaps the most joyous of all festivals, recalled with thanksgiving the experience of God's care in the wilderness. Celebrated at the end of the year, Ingathering signaled the conclusion of harvest-time and anticipated the beginning of a new agricultural cycle."

3. From *Ancient Christian Commentary on Scripture: Introduction and Biographic Information* (Downers Grove, IL: InterVarsity Press, 2005), 490, according to Cyril of Alexandria, patriarch of the region who was known for his astute biblical exegesis, "the two Emmaus disciples are not among the Eleven but could well be from among the seventy." (Here, "the seventy" refers to either the seventy or seventy-two additional disciples in addition to original twelve disciples whom Jesus trained in the "way of God" during his earthly ministry. Read the full account in Luke 10.)
4. See Colossians 1:15–21.

Session 3

1. See 2 Timothy 3:16–17.
2. See Deuteronomy 31:26.
3. See John 14:21–24.

Session 4

1. For a fun and family-friendly overview of this vital celebration in Jewish life, see What is Passover? - BBC Bitesize https://www.bbc.co.uk/bitesize/topics/znwhfg8/articles/zn22382
2. From the following site we learn that "Roman law allowed certain leaders to pardon prisoners as they saw fit. The gospels suggest a standing tradition existed in Judea in which the Roman governor would release one prisoner during the Passover celebration. Perhaps the prisoner was selected, at least in part, according to popular opinion. What Pilate does not realize—yet—is that the people present appear to have

been brought by Jesus' enemies to present a hostile scene (Matthew 27:20, 24; Mark 15:11, 15)": What does Matthew 27:15 mean? | BibleRef.com

Session 4 Solo Study

1. See Psalm 44:21; Proverbs 21:2; 1 Samuel 16:7; Jeremiah 17:10; and James 1:18.

Session 5

1. For a great article on the ancient-world threshing floor, see What is a Threshing Floor? Biblical Meaning for Christians (crosswalk.com). https://www.crosswalk.com/faith/bible-study/what-does-threshing-floor-mean-for-christians-today.html

Session 5 Solo Study

1. Harvard University recently released a fascinating and comprehensive study on loneliness as part of their "Making Caring Common" initiative, which can be found here: https://static1.squarespace.com/static/5b7c56e255b02c683659fe43/t/6021776bdd04957c4557c212/1612805995893/Loneliness+in+America+2021_02_08_FINAL.pdf (squarespace.com).

Session 6

1. See Matthew 16:25.
2. For more on the history of the book of Psalms, check out this stimulating synopsis from Pastor Chuck Swindoll, available both in audio or written form: Book of Psalms Overview - Insight for Living Ministries. https://insight.org/resources/bible/the-wisdom-books/psalms#:~:text=The%20book%20of%20Psalms%20expresses%20worship.%20Throughout%20its,us%20of%20the%20absolute%20centrality%20of%20His%20Word

ABOUT THE AUTHOR

Allison Allen attended Carnegie Mellon University's Acting Conservatory, and afterward landed on Broadway. She now uses her gifts to teach the Bible all over the country and loves nothing more than watching people run into the redemption that Jesus offers. Allison is the spiritual wingwoman to Lisa Harper on Lisa's well-received podcast, *Back Porch Theology*. She is the author of two books: *Shine* and *Thirsty for More*. Above all, she is grateful for the grace Christ offers to wonky-hearted people like herself.

From the Publisher

GREAT STUDIES

ARE EVEN BETTER WHEN THEY'RE SHARED!

Help others find this study:

- Post a review at your favorite online bookseller.
- Post a picture on a social media account and share why you enjoyed it.
- Send a note to a friend who would also love it—or, better yet, go through it with them.

Thanks for helping others grow their faith!